ULTIMATE POWER

NEGOTIATING
FOR SALESPEOPLE
MASTER COURSE

Also by Roger Dawson

The Secret to Achieving All Your Goals

ULTIMATE POWER

NEGOTIATING
FOR SALESPEOPLE
MASTER COURSE

ROGER DAWSON

MEDIA

MEDIA

Published 2023 by Gildan Media LLC
aka G&D Media
www.GandDmedia.com

FIRST EDITION 2023

Front Cover design by David Rheinhardt of Pyrographx

Interior design by Meghan Day Healey of Story Horse, LLC

Library of Congress Cataloging-in-Publication Data is available
upon request

ISBN: 978-1-7225-0650-6

10   9   8   7   6   5   4   3   2   1

Contents

Chapter One

Ask for the Max

Salespeople have been telling me that it's getting tougher out there. Buyers have more pressure on them than ever to get your price down. And they are much better negotiators than they were years ago.

Not so long ago, the slogan was, "Nothing happens until somebody sells something." We now have to amend that to "Nothing happens until somebody sells something *at a profit*!"

I hate to put it this bluntly, but here's what I think has happened: the companies to whom you sell have figured out that the best and quickest way for them to put money on their bottom line is to take it right off of yours.

Think about it for a moment: Your customers have three ways to improve their profits. The first way is to sell more, which means improving their market share by taking away some of their competitors' business or by creating new or different products and carving out a new market for themselves. But this is very risky and expensive. The second way is to reduce their operating expenses by firing employees or buying expensive new equipment. The third way is far easier: to do a better job negotiating with you and their other suppliers, to take money right off of your bottom line and put it directly onto theirs.

That's what General Motors decided to do in 2006, when they put Ignacio Lopez in charge of their buying operations. In the first six months on the job, he saved General Motors $2 billion by renegotiating contracts with suppliers. He took $2 billion from their suppliers' bottom lines and put it right onto GM's bottom line in six months.

Today companies are upgrading the position of buyer. Several years ago, you may have been selling to a buyer who only moved up through the ranks. Now you're dealing with someone who may have a master's degree in business or who has just come back from a

---

Customers have three ways to improve their profits

1. Sell More.
2. Reduce their operating expenses.
3. Do a better job negotiating with suppliers.

week-long negotiating course at Harvard University. Companies have found that doing a better job negotiating with you is a much easier way to improve their profits than increasing their market share or trying to shave more off their operating costs.

How do you as a salesperson respond to this assault on your company's profits and on your personal income? The answer is *power negotiating*. When you learn to become a power negotiator, you'll know how to get anything you want from the buyer and still have them thinking that they won. I don't mean tricking them into doing something they wouldn't do if they were smarter or better informed. Rather, I mean, always leaving the buyer with the permanent perception that they have won.

Impossible, you say? No, not to a power negotiator. As a salesperson, you've probably heard that the objective of a negotiation is to create a win-win solution, a creative way by which both you and the buyer can walk away from the negotiating table feeling that you've won.

There is the story of two people, both of whom want an orange but are frustrated because they only have one orange between them. They talk about it for a while, and they decide that to be fair, the best they can do is split the orange down the middle, each settling for half of what they really need.

But as these two people talk about their underlying needs in the negotiation, they find that one wants the orange to make juice, and the other needs the rind to bake a cake. They have magically found a way both of them can win and neither has to lose.

Sure—that could happen in the real world, but not enough to make it worthwhile. Let's face it. When you are sitting in front of a buyer, there's not going to be a magical win-win solution. He wants the lowest price and you want the highest price. He wants to take money right off of your bottom line and put it right onto his.

Power negotiating takes a different position. Power negotiating teaches you how to win at the negotiating table but leave the buyer thinking that he or she won. In fact, I'd almost give that to you as a definition of a power negotiator.

Two salespeople might go out to meet with two buyers who are in exactly the same circumstances. Both salespeople might close the sale at exactly the same price and terms, but the power negotiator comes away with the buyer feeling that they have won. The poor negotiator comes away with the buyer feeling that they have lost.

I'll teach you how to negotiate in such a way that the buyer permanently feels that they won. They won't wake up the next morning thinking, "Now I know what that salesperson did to me. Wait till I see him again." No, they'll be thinking about what a great time they had negotiating with you and how they can't wait to see you again.

If you'll learn and apply the secrets of power negotiating that I'll teach you in this book, you'll never again feel that you've lost to a buyer. You'll always come away from the negotiating table knowing that you've won and knowing that you have improved your relationship with the buyer.

Overstate Your Demands

Let's start out by talking about one of the most important things you can learn about power negotiating: *ask the buyer for more than you expect to get.* Henry Kissinger went so far as to say, "Effectiveness at the conference table depends on overstating one's demands." Isn't that interesting? One of the world's great international negotiators says that if you are planning to negotiate with him, you should expect him to ask for more than he thinks he'll get from you. Remember that if you were thinking, "My buyers are not stupid: they'll know the minute I ask for more than I expect to get." Even if that were so, it's still an excellent negotiating principle.

Think of some reasons why you should ask for more than you expect to get. Why should you ask for fullest price even if you know that it's higher than the buyer's paying? Why should you ask the buyer to invest in the top-of-the-line even when you are convinced that they're so budget-conscious that they'll never spend that much? Why should you assume that they'll want to buy

Effectiveness at the conference table
depends on *overstating* one's demands.
—Henry Kissinger

your extended service warranty even though you know they've never done that in the past?

If you've thought about this, you probably came up with a couple of good reasons to ask for more than you expect to get. The obvious answer is that it gives you some negotiating room.

You can always come down, but you can never go up on price (although when we get to ending negotiating gambits in a later chapter, I'll show you how to nibble for more: some things are easier to get at the end of the negotiation than they are at the beginning).

You should be asking for your MPP, your *maximum plausible position*. This is the most that you can ask for and still have the buyer sees some plausibility in your position. The less you know about the other side, the higher your initial position should be, for two reasons: The first reason is that you may be off in your assumptions. If you don't know the buyer or their needs, they may be willing to pay more than you think. The second reason, if this is a new relationship, is that you'll appear much more cooperative if you're able to make larger concessions. The better you know the buyer and their needs, the more you can modify your position. Conversely, if the other side doesn't know you, their initial demands may be more outrageous.

If you are asking for far more than your maximum plausible position, imply some flexibility. If your initial position seems outrageous to the buyer and your attitude is "take it or leave it," you may not even get the negotiations started. The buyer may simply respond, "Then we don't have anything to talk about."

But you can get away with an outrageous opening position if you imply some flexibility. You might say, "We may be able to modify this position once we know more precisely about your needs, but based on what we know so far about the quantities you will be ordering, the quality of the packaging, and you not needing just-in-time inventory, our best price would be about $2.25 per widget." The buyer will probably be thinking, "That's outrageous, but he does seem flexible, so I'll spend some time negotiating with him, and I'll see how low I can get him to go."

Here's the problem for you as a salesperson: your real MPP is probably much higher than you think it is. We all fear being ridiculed by the other side (which is something that I'll talk more about in a later chapter, when we discuss coercive power). We're all reluctant to take a position that will cause the buyer to laugh at us or put us down. Over the years, you have probably modified your MPP to the point where you are asking for far less than the maximum price that the buyer would think is plausible. To give you greater confidence, let me identify five reasons that you should ask for your MPP—for more than you expect to get. The first reason is that it gives you some negotiating room. You can always come down, but you can never come up.

If you're a positive thinker, the second reason for asking for more than you expect to get will be obvious to you: you might just get it. You don't know how the universe is aligned that day.

Perhaps the patron saint of salespeople is leaning over a cloud, looking down at you, and thinking, "Wow, look at that salesperson for XYZ Industries. She's been working so hard for so long. Now let's just give her a break!"

The third reason to ask for more than you expect to get is that it raises the perceived value of your product or service. When you show the buyer your printed price list, in his or her mind it imparts a subliminal value to the item. Obviously, the effect is greater with an inexperienced buyer than it is with a seasoned pro, but the effect is always there.

The fourth reason for asking for your MPP is that it's a great strategy for avoiding deadlocks caused by conflicting egos of the negotiators. Take a look at the Gulf War in 1990–91. (You do remember the Gulf War? It was on CNN.) Saddam Hussein, the dictator of Iraq, had invaded Kuwait. What were we asking Saddam Hussein to do? (Perhaps asking is not exactly the right word.) President George H.W. Bush, in his State of the Union address, described our opening negotiating position with a beautiful piece of alliteration: "I'm not bragging, I'm not bluffing, and I'm not bullying. But there are three things this man has to do. He has to get out of Kuwait. He has to restore the legitimate government of Kuwait instead of installing a puppet government, as the Soviets did when they left Afghanistan. And he has to make reparations for the damage that he's done."

That was a very clear and precise opening negotiating position. The problem was that this was also our bottom line; it was the *least* for which we would settle. No wonder the situation deadlocked. It had to deadlock because we didn't give Saddam Hussein room to preserve his ego. If we'd said, "We want you and all your cronies exiled. We want a neutral, non-Arab government installed in Baghdad. We want UN supervision of the removal of all military capability. In addition, we want you out of Kuwait, the legitimate Kuwaiti government restored, and reparation for the damages that you did." Then we could have gotten what we wanted and still let Saddam Hussein salvage his ego.

I know what you're thinking: "Saddam Hussein was not on my Christmas card list last year. I don't care if his ego deflates." Why should the United States have asked for more than it wanted?

Because in that situation, there's no way that the other party can negotiate with you and feel that they've won.

Inexperienced negotiators always want to start with their best offer. This is the salesperson who wants to announce that they've won in the negotiations. But particularly with egotistical buyers, always leave some room to let them have a win. So the fifth reason to ask for your MPP is that it creates a climate where the other side can win.

Power negotiators always ask for more than they expect to get. Let's recap the five reasons for asking for more than you expect to get.

> ### Five reasons for asking for more than you expect to get.
>
> 1. It gives you some negotiating room. You can always come down, but you can never go up.
> 2. You might just get it.
> 3. It raises the perceived value of your product or service.
> 4. It avoids deadlocks caused by conflicting egos of the negotiators.
> 5. It creates a climate where the other side can win.

Ask for more than you expect to get. It seems like such an obvious principle, but it has proven itself over and over again. The more you ask for, the more you're going to get.

When the buyer is asking you for more than he expects to get, the counter-gambit is to recognize the game: "I could respond with an equally outrageous proposal, but neither of us would benefit from that approach. Why don't you tell me the highest price you can live with, and I'll take it to my people?"

That's a good assumption to make. If you don't have anything else on which to go, assume that you'll end up in the middle between the two opening negotiating positions. In both little and big situations, you will be amazed by how often this happens.

In little things: Your son comes to you and says he needs $100 for a fishing trip he's going to take this weekend. You say, "No way. I'm not going to give you

> An obvious principle of negotiating:
> *The more you ask for, the more you are going to get.*

$100. Do you realize that when I was your age, I got an allowance of 50 cents a week? I had to work for that. I'll give you $50 and not a penny more."

In 1986, the Reagan administration asked Mexico to contribute huge amounts of petroleum to the US strategic petroleum reserve. We proposed to the Mexicans that they pay us a $100 million negotiating fee. When Mexican president José López Portillo heard what we were asking for, he went ballistic. He said the equivalent of, "You tell Ronald Reagan to drop dead. We're not paying the United States a negotiating fee, not one peso, nada."

So here we have the negotiating range established. We were asking for $100 million. Mexico was offering zero. Guess what they ended up paying us? That's right: $50 million. How much do you think they would've paid us if we'd asked for $50 million? You got it: probably $25 million. In both little and big things, we end up splitting the difference. With bracketing power, negotiators are assured that if that happens, they still get what they want.

Get the Other Side to Commit First
Bracketing assumes that you've gotten the other side to state their position first. That principle is one of the

five most important things to learn about power negotiating: *get the other side to commit first*. Don't let the
buyer say to you, "You just give us your best price, and
we'll tell you whether we'll accept it or not." He's saying, "You make a commitment to us, but we are not
going to make any commitment to you at all." That's a
wonderful negotiating position for the buyer, but it's a
terrible position for you. You'd be better off if the buyer
said, "I want you to give it to me" than, "You just give
me your lowest price, and I'll tell you if I'll take it or
not." If the buyer can get you to state your position first,
they can bracket you so that if you end up splitting the
differences (as often happens), the buyer ends up getting what they want. This is another underlying principle of negotiating that I'll get back to later: *get the other
side to state their position first*. It may not be as bad as
you fear, and it's necessary so that you can bracket their
proposal.

Don't let the other side trick you into committing
first. If the status quo is fine with you and there's no
pressure on you to make a move, be bold enough to say
to the other side, "I'm satisfied with the way things are.
You are the one who approached me. If you want to do
this, you'll have to make a proposal to me."

If Paul McCartney had learned to avoid making the
first offer, he'd be even richer today. In the early days of
the Beatles, their manager, Brian Epstein, was negotiating a contract for their first movie. United Artists had
planned it as a teenage exploitation movie and budgeted
only $300,000. The producer offered Epstein $25,000

and a percentage of the profits. United Artists was willing to pay up to 25 percent of the profits if the Beatles would agree to the token cash payment. The studio negotiator was good enough to play his hand close to the vest, without revealing his position. He asked Brian Epstein what he wanted first. Brian was not used to big numbers yet and hadn't taken the time to research the industry. He assertively replied that he wouldn't accept a penny less than 7.5 percent. The movie, *A Hard Day's Night*, was an international success. Brian's error of making the first offer cost the Beatles millions.

Another benefit to bracketing is that it tells you how big your concessions can be as the negotiation progresses. Let's go back to the widget sales situation. The buyer has told you that he can't go a penny over $1.60. You've told the buyer that your company would be losing money at a penny less than $1.80. Your goal is to get to $1.70. The buyer comes up to $1.63. You can move down now to $1.77, and your goal—$1.70—will still be in the middle of the two proposals that are on the negotiating table. In that way, you can move in on your target and know that if the other side offer to split the difference, you can still make your goal. However, don't forget what I told you earlier: if you go in with a ridiculously high offer, you might scare the buyer off by being too forceful. If you start out by saying, "Our list price on widgets is $1.80, and the only time we ever deviate from that is for carload quantities," you may offend the buyer with such a high price that he or she won't even start negotiating with you.

My advice is to go in high, but imply flexibility in the offer. You might say, "Our list price is $1.80, but if you are prepared to give me a substantial part of your business, I may be able to do better. What would it take to get a major commitment from you?" So rather than go in with $1.80 offer and implying, "Take it or leave it," you're better off to imply flexibility. Your price may be high, but because you are indicating a willingness to negotiate, the buyer tends to think, "I can get them down from that. Why don't I spend some time and see if I can get them down to a lower price than I'm paying now?" It's a better way to get the negotiations started.

The counter-gambit to bracketing is to prevent the buyer from being able to do it to you by getting him to commit to a position first. If you don't state your position first, the buyer can't bracket you.

Let's recap the key points about bracketing:

1. Assume that you'll end up midway between the two opening negotiating positions.
2. You can only bracket if you get the buyer to state his or her position first.
3. Continue bracketing as you make concessions.

In the next chapter, I'll teach you how to deal with the buyer who is grinding away on you for a better deal. I'll also teach you how to deal with the buyer who doesn't appear to want what you are selling.

In this chapter, I've taught you three of the most important things you can learn about negotiating the sale:

1. Ask for more than you expect to get.
2. Get the buyer to commit to a position before you do.
3. Bracket your objective so that if you end up in the middle, you get what you want.

Chapter Two

Turn Down the First Offer

In the previous chapter, we talked about three of the most important principles in sales negotiation. Now I'll teach you three more key principles:

1. Why you should never say yes to the first offer.
2. Why you should always flinch at the buyer's suggestions.
3. How to deal with a buyer who doesn't appear to want what you're selling.

Never Say Yes to the First Offer

You should never do this, because it automatically triggers two thoughts in the buyer's mind. Put yourself in the buyer's shoes for a moment. Let's say that you're the buyer for a maker of aircraft engines, and you're about to meet with a salesperson who represents a manufacturer of engine bearings—a vital component for you. Your regular supplier has let you down, and you need to make an emergency purchase from this new company. They are the only people who can supply the product within the thirty days that you need to prevent a shutdown of your assembly line. If you can't supply the engines on time, it will invalidate your contract with the aircraft manufacturer that gives you 85 percent of your business.

Under these circumstances, the price of the bearings you need is definitely not a high priority. However, as your secretary announces the arrival of the salesperson, you think, "I'll be a good negotiator just to see what happens. I'll make him a super-low offer."

The salesperson makes his presentation and assures you that he can ship on time to your specifications. He quotes you a price of $250 each for the bearings. This surprises you, because you've been paying $275 for them. But you manage to mask your surprise and respond with, "We've only been paying $175," to which the salesperson responds, "OK, we can match that."

At this point you almost certainly have two responses: 1. "I could have done better"; 2. "Something must be wrong." In the thousands of seminars that I've conducted over the years, I've posed a situation like this to audiences, and I can't recall getting anything other than these two responses.

. . . .

When you say "yes" to the first offer,
you almost always have two responses:
1. I could have done better;
2. Something must be wrong.

. . . .

Let's look at each of these responses separately. First reaction: "I could have done better." Note that this doesn't have a thing to do with the price. It only has to do with the way the other person reacts to the proposal. What if the bearing salesperson had agreed to $150 or $125? Wouldn't you still think that you could have done better?

A number of years ago, I bought a hundred acres of land in Eatonville, Washington, a beautiful little town just west of Mount Rainier. The seller was asking $185,000 for the land. I analyzed the property and decided that if I could get it for $150,000, it would be a terrific buy. I bracketed that price, and I asked the real estate agent to present an offer to the seller at $115,050. (Specific numbers build credibility, so you are more likely to get them to accept this offer rather than countering at a higher price.) I went back to La Habra Heights, California, where I lived, leaving the agent to present the offer to the seller. Frankly, I thought I'd be lucky if they responded with any kind of counteroffer on a proposal this low.

To my amazement, I got the offer back in the mail a few days later, accepted at the price and terms that

I had proposed. I know that I got a terrific buy on the land. Within a year, I had sold sixty of the acres for more than I paid for the whole hundred. Later I sold another twenty acres for more than I paid for the whole hundred.

When the seller accepted my offer, I should have been thinking, "Wow, that's terrific. I couldn't have gotten a lower price." That's what I should have been thinking, but I wasn't. I was thinking, "I could have done better." It doesn't have anything to do with the price: it only has to do with the way the other side reacts to the proposal.

My second reaction when I received the accepted offer on the land was, "Something must be wrong. I'm going to take a thorough look at the preliminary appraiser's report when it comes in."

Similarly, the second thought that the buyer of the bearings will have is, "Something must be wrong. Maybe something's changed in the market since I last negotiated a bearing contract. Instead of going ahead, I think I'll tell this salesperson that I've got to check with a committee and then talk to some other suppliers."

These two reactions will go through anybody's mind if they say yes to the first offer. Let's say that your son came to you and said, "Could I borrow the car tonight?" and you said, "Sure, son, take it; have a wonderful time." Wouldn't he automatically think, "I could have done better? I could have gotten $10 out of this." And wouldn't he also think, "What's going on here? How come they want me out of the house? What's going on that I don't understand?"

Refusing to jump at the first offer is a very easy negotiating principle to understand, but it's very hard to remember when you are in the thick of a negotiation. You may have formed a mental picture of how you expect the buyer to respond, and that is a dangerous thing to do. Napoleon Bonaparte once said, "The unforgivable sin of a commander is to assume that the enemy will act in a certain way in a given situation when his response may be altogether different." You are expecting the other party to counter at a ridiculous figure, but to your surprise, the buyer's proposal is much more reasonable than you expected.

Power negotiators are careful to avoid the trap of saying yes too quickly. They want to keep the other party from thinking either that they could have done better or that something is wrong. A sophisticated buyer won't tell you that he felt that he lost in the negotiation, but he will tuck it away in the back of his mind, thinking, "The next time I deal with a salesperson, I'll be a tough negotiator. I won't leave any money on the table next time."

Turning down the first offer may be tough to do, particularly if you've been calling on the buyer for months and they come through with a proposal just as you're about to give up. When this happens, it will tempt you to grab what you can. But be a power negotiator. Remember not to say yes too quickly.

I used to think that it was a 100 percent rule that you should never say yes to the first offer until I heard from a real estate office manager in Los Angeles who told me, "I was driving down Hollywood Boulevard last night, listening to your audio program in my car. I stopped at the gas station to use the restroom. When I came back to my car, somebody stuck a gun in my ribs and said, 'OK, buddy, give me your wallet.'

"I'd just been listening to your recording, so I said, 'Here's what I'm prepared to do. I'll give you the cash, but let me keep the wallet and the credit cards. Fair enough?'

"And he said, 'Buddy, you didn't listen to me, did you? Give me the wallet.'"

Sometimes you should say yes to the first offer, but it's almost a 100 percent rule that you shouldn't.

The counter-gambit to never jumping in at the first offer is to protect yourself with higher authority. Always be thinking to yourself, "Whatever the buyer's counter-proposal may be, I can't accept it. I have to take it to my committee."

Key points to remember

1. Never say yes to the first offer or counteroffer.
2. The biggest danger is when you've formed a mental picture of how the buyer will respond to your proposal and they come back much higher than you expected.

Prepare for these possibilities so they won't catch you off guard.

Flinching

The next gambit I want to teach you will sound silly when I first tell you about it, but don't let its simplicity fool you. It's very powerful. I have more people tell me about their success with this than any other gambit I teach. It's called *flinching*.

Power negotiators know that you should always flinch, which means to react with shock and surprise at the buyer's proposals. Let's say that you're in a resort area and watch a charcoal sketch artist at work. He doesn't have the price posted. You ask him how much he charges, and he tells you, "$15." If that doesn't appear to shock you, his next words will be, "And $5 extra for color." If you still don't appear to be shocked, he'll say, "And we have these shipping kits here; you'll need one of these too."

With a flinch, when he tells you the price, you counter with "$15! That's a lot of money."

"Well, I'll tell you what I will do," he'll say. "I'll normally charge $5 extra for the color, but for you, I'll throw it in at no extra charge.

"That's still a lot of money," you say.

"Well, come here," he says. "I have never done this before, but you are such a nice person that I'll not only throw in the color but I'll give you one of these shipping kits too."

See the difference. Perhaps you know someone who would never flinch like that because they think it's beneath their dignity. This kind of person would walk

> Power Negotiating Gambit—*Flinching*: To react
> with shock and surprise at the buyer's proposals.

into a store and ask, "How much is the coat in the window?" The clerk would respond, "$2,000." "That's not bad," they'll say. I would be in the background, having a heart attack.

I know it sounds dumb, and I know it sounds ridiculous, but the truth of the matter is that when the buyers make a proposal to you, they are watching for your reaction.

They may not think for a moment that you'll agree to their request. They've just thrown it out to see what your reaction will be. For example, you sell computers, and the buyer asks you to include an extended warranty. You sell cars, and the buyer asks you to include free floor mats and a tank of gas. You sell contractor supplies, and the buyer asks you to deliver it to the job site at no extra charge. You sell fax machines, and the buyer asks you to include a year's supply of paper.

In each of these situations, the buyer may not have thought for a moment that you would go along with his request, but if you don't flinch, he or she will automatically think, "Maybe I will get them to go along with that. I didn't think they would, but I think I'll be a tough negotiator and see how far I can get them to go."

It's very interesting to observe a negotiation when you know what both sides are thinking. Wouldn't you

love to know what's going on in the buyer's mind when
you're negotiating with them? When I conduct my seminars, we break up into groups and do some negotiating to practice the principles that I teach. I create a
workshop and customize it to the industry in which the
participants are involved. If they're medical equipment
salespeople, they may find themselves negotiating the
sale of laser surgery equipment to a hospital. If they're
printing salespeople, the workshop may involve the
acquisition of a smaller printing company in an outly-
ing town. I break the audience up into buyers, sellers,
and referees.

The referees are in a very interesting position,
because they have been in on the planning sessions of
both the buyers and the sellers. They know each side's
negotiating range. They know what the opening offer is
going to be, and they know how far each side will go.
The sellers of the printing company would go as low as
$700,000, but they may start as high as $2 million. The
buyers may start at $400,000, but they're willing to go
to $1.5 million if they have to. We call that the *high* and
the *low* of each side's negotiating range. Hopefully, the
high end of the buyer's negotiating range is more than
the low end of the seller's negotiating range. We call the
extent to which the two negotiating ranges overlap the
acceptance range. The combined negotiating range of
the buyers and sellers is $400,000 to $2 million, but the
acceptance range is $700,000 to $1.5 million.

The negotiating starts with each side trying to get
the other side to put their offer on the table first. After

a while, somebody has to break the ice. The seller suggests the $2 million: the top of their negotiating range. In their mind, $2 million is ridiculously high, and they barely have the nerve to propose it; they think they're going to get laughed out of the room the minute they do. They expect the buyers to say, "You want us to do what? You must be out of your minds!" However, to their surprise, the buyers don't appear to be that shocked: their response is much milder—perhaps, "We don't think we are prepared to go that high."

In an instant, the negotiation changes. Just a moment ago, the sellers were thinking that $2 million was an impossible goal. Now they're thinking that perhaps they're not as far apart as they thought they were. Now they're thinking, "Let's hang in. Let's be tough negotiators. Maybe we will get this much."

Flinching is critical because most people believe more what they see than what they hear. In most people, the visual overrides the auditory. It's safe to assume that at least 70 percent of your buyers will be visuals: what they see is more important than what they hear.

I'm sure that you've had some exposure to Neuro-linguistic programming (NLP). You know that people are either visual, auditory, or kinesthetic. There are a few gustatory (taste) and olfactory (smell) people out there, but not many, and they are chefs or perfume makers, not negotiators.

**Three processing modes of
Neuro-Linguistic Programming (NLP)**
1. Visual—see a picture of a memory
2. Auditory—hear a memory
3. Kinesthetic—getting a "feeling" of a memory

If you'd like to know which you are, close your eyes for ten seconds and think of the house you lived in when you were ten years old. You probably saw the house in your mind, so you are a visual. Perhaps you didn't get a good visual picture, but you heard what was going on—trains passing by or children playing: that means you're auditory.

Some auditories are *very* auditory. Neil Berman is a psychotherapist friend of mine in Santa Fe, New Mexico. He can remember every conversation he's ever had with a patient, but if he meets them in the supermarket, he doesn't remember them. The minute they say, "Good morning" to him, he thinks, "Oh yes, that's the bipolar personality with antisocial tendencies."

The final possibility is that you didn't so much see or hear but just got a feeling for what it was like when you were ten. That makes you a kinesthetic.

Unless you have something else to go on, assume that people are visual. That's the importance of flinching in response to a proposal. Don't dismiss flinching as too childish or theatrical until you've had a chance to see how effective it can be.

The effectiveness of flinching always surprises my students when they first use it. One woman told me that she flinches when selecting a bottle of wine in one of Boston's finest restaurants, and the wine steward immediately dropped the price by $5. A man told me that a simple flinch caused a salesperson to take $2,000 off the price of a Corvette. A speaker friend of mine attended my seminar in Orange County, California, and decided to see if he could use it to get his speaking fees up. At the time, he was just getting started and was charging $1,500. He went to a company and proposed that they hire him to do some in-house training. The training director said, "We might be interested in having you work for us, but the most we can pay you is $1,500."

In the past, my friend would have said, "That's what I charge. But now he gasped in surprise and said, $1,500! I can't afford to do it for $1,500!" The training director frowned thoughtfully and said, "Well, the most we've ever offered any speaker is $2,500. So that's the very best we can do."

That meant $1,000 of additional profit per speech to my friend, and it only took him fifteen seconds to do it—not bad pay.

The counter-gambit to the flinch is to smile and recognize the gambit: "That was a terrific flinch. Where did you learn how to do that?" If he tells you that it was from reading this book, you'll have a lot in common, won't you?

Key points to flinching in reaction to a proposal

1. They may not expect to get what they're asking for. If you don't show surprise, you're communicating that it's a possibility.
2. A concession often follows a flinch. If you don't flinch, it makes the buyer a tough negotiator.
3. Assume that the buyer is visual unless you have something else to go on.
4. Even if you're not face-to-face with a buyer, you can still gasp in shock and surprise, because phone flinches can also be very effective.

The Reluctant Seller

Now let me teach you how to play reluctant seller and defend yourself against the reluctant buyer. Imagine for a moment that you own a sailboat and you are desperate to sell it. It was fun when you first got it, but now you hardly ever use it, and the maintenance and slip fees are eating you alive. It's early Sunday morning, and you've given up the chance to play golf with your buddies because you need to be down at the marina cleaning your boat. You're scrubbing away and cursing your stupidity for even having bought it.

Just as you're thinking, "I'm going to give this turkey away to the next person who comes along," you look up and see an expensively dressed, silver-haired man with a young girl on his arm coming down the dock.

He's wearing Gucci loafers, white slacks, and a blue Burberry blazer topped off with a silk cravat. His young girlfriend is wearing high heels, a silk sheath dress, big sunglasses, and huge diamond earrings. They stop at your boat, and the man says, "That's a fine-looking boat, young man; by any chance is it for sale?"

His girlfriend snuggles up to him and says, "Oh, let's buy it, Popsy; we'll have so much fun."

You feel your heart starting to burst with joy, and your mind is singing: "Thank you, Jesus! Thank you, Jesus!"

Expressing that sentiment is not going to get you the best price for your boat, is it? How are you going to get the best price?

One of the most effective ways to get the best price, is by playing reluctant seller. You keep on scrubbing and say, "You're welcome to come onboard, although I hadn't thought of selling the boat." You give them a tour of the boat and at every step of the way, you tell them how much you love the boat and how much fun you have sailing her. Finally, you tell them, "I can see how perfect this boat would be for you and how much fun you'd have with it, but I really don't think that I could ever bear to part with it. However, just to be fair to you, what is the very best price you would give me?"

Power negotiators know that this reluctant seller technique squeezes the negotiating range before the negotiation even starts. If you've done a good job of building the other person's desire to own the boat, they will have formed a negotiating range in their mind.

They may be thinking, "I'd be willing to go to $30,000, $25,000 would be a fair deal, and $20,000 would be a bargain." So their negotiating range is from $20,000 to $30,000. Just by playing reluctant seller, you will have moved them up through that range. If you'd appeared eager to sell, they might have offered you $20,000 by playing reluctant buyer. You may have moved them up to the midpoint or even the high point of their negotiating range before the negotiations even start.

One of my power negotiators is an extremely rich and powerful investor, a man who owns real estate all over town. He probably owns real estate worth $50 million, owes $35 million in loans, and therefore has a net worth of about $15 million. Very successful—what you might justifiably call a heavy hitter. Like many investors, he likes wheeling and dealing. His strategy is simple: buy a property at the right price and on the right terms, hold on to it, let it appreciate, and then sell at a higher price. Many smaller investors bring him purchase offers for one of his buildings, eager to acquire one of his better-known properties. When that happens, he always uses the reluctant seller gambit. He reads the offer quietly, and when he's finished, slides it thoughtfully back across the desk, saying, "I don't know. Of all my properties, I have very special feelings for this one. I was thinking of keeping it and giving it to my daughter for her college graduation present. I really don't think that I would part for it for anything less than the full asking price. You understand, this particular property is worth a great deal to me, but look, it was good of you to bring an offer for me. In all fairness, so that you won't have wasted your time, what is the very best price you would give me?" Many times I have seen him make thousands in just a few seconds using the reluctant seller philosophy.

Power negotiators always try to edge up the other side's negotiating range before the real negotiating ever begins, so power negotiators always play reluctant seller when they're selling. It squeezes the negotiating range before the negotiation even starts.

Now let's turn this around and consider the reluctant buyer. Put yourself on the other side of the desk for a moment. If you were the purchasing agent, how would you get a salesperson to give you the lowest possible price? If I were a purchasing agent, I would let the salesperson come in and have them go through their entire presentation. I would ask all the questions I could possibly think of, and when finally I couldn't think of another thing to ask, I would say, "I really appreciate all the time that you've taken. You've obviously put a lot of work into this presentation, but unfortunately, it's just not the way we want to go, but I sure wish you the best of luck."

I would pause to admire the crestfallen expression on the salesperson's face. I would watch him slowly package up his presentation materials with a heavy heart. Then at the very last minute, just as his hand hit the doorknob on the way out, I would come back with this magic expression. (There are some magic expressions in negotiating. If you use them at exactly the right moment, the predictability of the other side's response is amazing.) I would say, "You know, I really do appreciate the time you took with me. Just to be fair to you, what is the very lowest price that you would take?"

It's a good bet that the first price the salesperson quoted is not the real bottom line. The first price a salesperson quotes is what I call the *wish number*. This is what they are wishing the buyer would do. If the buyer said OK to that, they would probably burn rubber all the way back to their sales office running and screaming.

The first price quoted is the wish price. There is also the walkaway price—a price at which the salesperson will not or cannot sell. The buyer doesn't know what the walkaway price is, so they have to probe for information. They have to try some negotiating gambits to see if they can figure out the salesperson's walkaway price.

When the purchasing agent plays reluctant buyer, the salesperson is not going to come all the way down from the wish price to the walkaway price. However, here is what will typically happen when the purchasing agent plays reluctant buyer: the salesperson will typically give away half of his negotiating range. If a furniture salesperson has a wish price of $225,000,

....

The *wish number*:
The first price a salesperson quotes.

....

knowing that his bottom line is $175,000, he will typically respond to the reluctant buyer with, "Well, I tell you what. It's the end of our quarter, and we're in a sales contest. If you'll place the order today, I'll give it to you for the unbelievably low price of $200,000." He'll give away half of his negotiating range just because the purchasing agent played reluctant buyer.

When buyers do this kind of thing to you, it's just a game that they're playing. Power negotiators don't get upset about it. They've just learned to play the negotiating game better than the other party.

The counter-gambit to a reluctant buyer is to say, "I don't think that there is any flexibility in the price, but if you'll tell me what it would take to get your business"—getting the other side to commit first—"I'll take it to my people." (Use the higher authority and middle negotiating gambit, which I'll cover later.) "I'll see what I can do for you with them."

In this chapter, you've learned that you should never say yes to the first offer. You've been taught how to flinch at the other party's proposals and how to play reluctant buyer and deal with a reluctant seller.

In the next chapter, I'll teach you how to squeeze concessions out of the buyer with the vise technique, why you should never offer to split the difference, and what to do when the buyer says, "We don't have it in the budget."

**Key points to remember about reluctant buyer
and reluctant seller**

1. Always play reluctant seller.
2. Look out for the reluctant buyer.
3. Playing the reluctance gambit is a great way to
   squeeze the other side's negotiating range before
   the negotiation even starts.
4. The other side will typically give away half of their
   negotiating range just because you use this gambit.

Chapter Three

The Vise and Splitting the Difference

I n this chapter, I'll teach you three more key principles: (1) the vise technique, a simple phrase that will
make you a lot of money; (2) why you should never
offer to split the difference; and (3) what to do when the
buyer says, "We don't have it in the budget."

The Vise Technique

First, let me tell you about the vise. What it will do for
you will amaze you. The vise is a simple little expression: *you'll have to do better than that.*

Here's how power negotiators use it. The buyer
has listened to your proposal and your pricing struc-

. . . .

The "Vise" Technique:
"You'll have to do better than that."

. . . .

ture. You've ignored his insistence that he's happy with his present supplier and done a good job of building desire for your product. Finally, the buyer says to you, "I'm really happy with our present vendor, but I guess it wouldn't do any harm to have a backup supplier to keep them on their toes. I'll take one carload if you can get the price down to $1.22 per pound."

You respond with the vise. You calmly say, "I'm sorry, you'll have to do better than that."

You've made your proposal and then shut up. The buyer may just say yes, so it's foolish to say a word until you find out if he or she will accept your proposal.

I once watched two salespeople do the silent close on each other. There were three of us sitting at a circular conference table. The salesman on my right wanted to buy a piece of real estate from the salesman on my left. He made his proposal and then shut up, just as they had taught him in sales training school. The more experienced sales person on my left must have thought, "Son of a gun. I can't believe this. He's going to try the silent close on *me*. I'll teach him a lesson. I won't talk either."

So there I was, faced with two strong-willed people who were both sitting there daring the other to be the next one to talk. I didn't know how this was ever going to get resolved. There was a dead silence in the room except for the grandfather clock ticking away in the background.

I looked at each of them; obviously they both knew what was going on, and neither one was willing to give in to the other. I didn't know how it would ever get resolved. It seemed as though half an hour went by, although it was probably more like five minutes.

Finally, the more experienced salesperson broke the impasse by scrawling the word *decizion* on a pad of paper and sliding it across the table to the other salesperson. He had deliberately misspelled the word, using a Z instead of an S. The younger salesperson looked at it, and without thinking said, "You misspelled *decision*." Once he started talking, he couldn't stop. (Do you know a salesperson like that? Once they start talking, they can't stop.) He went on to say, "If you're not willing to accept what I offered you, I might be willing to come up another $2,000, but not a penny more."

He renegotiated his own proposal before he found out if the other person would accept it or not.

To use the vise technique, power negotiators simply respond to the other side's proposal or counterproposal with, "I'm sorry, you'll have to do better than that," and then shut up.

A client of mine called me and said, "Roger, I thought you might like to know that we just made $14,000 using one of the gambits that you taught us. We were having new equipment put into our Miami office. Our standard procedure has been to get three bids from qualified vendors and then take the lowest bid. So I was sitting here going over the bids. I was just about to OK the one I decided to accept; then I remembered what you taught me about the vise technique. So I thought, 'What have I got to lose?' and scrawled across it, 'You'll have to do better than this," and mailed it back to them. Their counterproposal came back $14,000 less than the proposal that I would have accepted."

Now you may be thinking, "Roger, you didn't tell us whether that was a $50,000 proposal—in which case it would have been a huge concession—or a multimillion-dollar proposal, in which case it wouldn't have been that big a deal." Don't fall into the trap of negotiating percentages when you should be negotiating dollars. The point was that this man made $14,000 in the two minutes that it took him to scroll that counterproposal across the bid, which meant that while he was doing it, he was generating $420,000 per hour of bottom-line profits. That's pretty good money, isn't it?

This is a trap into which attorneys fall. When I work with attorneys, it's very clear that if they're negotiating a $50,000 lawsuit, they might send a letter back and forth over $5,000. If it's a million-dollar lawsuit, they'll kick $50,000 around as though it doesn't mean a thing, because they're mentally negotiating percentages, not dollars. But if you make a $2,000 concession to a buyer, it doesn't matter if you made it to get a $10,000 sale or a million-dollar sale: it's still $2,000 that you've given away. It doesn't make any sense for you to come back to your sales manager and say, "I had to make a $2,000 concession, but it's a $100,000 sale." You should have been thinking, "There was $2,000 sitting in the middle of the negotiating table. How much more time should I be willing to spend to see how much more of it I could get?"

Have a feel for what your time's worth. Don't spend half an hour negotiating a $10 item unless you're just doing it for the practice. Even if you got them to concede all of the $10, you'd only be making money at the rate of $20 an hour.

To put this in perspective, if you make $100,000 a year, you are making about $50 an hour. So you should be thinking yourself, "Is what I'm doing right now generating more than $50 an hour?" If so, it's part of the solution. If you are aimlessly chatting with someone at the water cooler or straightening up your desk or anything else that is not generating $50 an hour, it's part of the problem.

Here's the point: When you're negotiating with a buyer and hang in a little bit longer and do a little bit better, you are not making $50 an hour; you're making $50 a minute, probably $50 a second. If that's not enough, remember that a negotiated dollar is a bottom-line dollar; it's not a gross sales dollar. So the $2,000 that you may have conceded in seconds because you thought it was the only way you could make the sale is worth many times that in gross sales dollars.

I've trained executives at discount retailers and health maintenance organizations, HMOs, where the profit margin is only 2 percent. They do $1 billion with a business a year, but they only bring in 2 percent in bottom-line profits. So at their company, a $2,000 concession at the negotiating table has the same impact on the bottom line as getting a $100,000 sale. You're probably in an industry that does better than that. I train people at some companies where the bottom line is an incredible 25 percent of the gross sales, but that's the exception: in this country, the average profit margin is 5 percent of gross sales. So that $2,000 concession you made is probably the equivalent of making a $40,000 sale.

So, let me ask you: how long would you be willing to work to get a $40,000 sale? An hour? Two hours? All day? I've had many sales managers tell me, "For a $40,000 sale, I expect my salespeople to work as long as it takes." However fast-paced your business, you're probably willing to spend several hours to make a $40,000 sale. So why are you so willing to make a $2,000 concession at the negotiating table? It has the same impact on the bottom line as a $40,000 sale, if your business generates the typical 5 percent bottom line profit. A negotiated dollar is a bottom-line dollar.

I don't care if you do brain surgery in your spare time: you'll never make money faster than you will when you're negotiating. So power negotiators always respond to a proposal with, *you'll have to do better than that*.

The counter-gambit to the vise, when the buyer uses it on you, is to automatically respond with, "Exactly how much better than that do I have to do?" This is an attempt to get the buyer pinned down to a position. You should never make a concession to a buyer unless it's in response to a specific counterproposal from them.

Key points to remember about the vise gambit

1. Respond to the proposal or counterproposal with the vise gambit: "You'll have to do better than that."

2. If it's used on you, respond with the counter-gambit: "Exactly how much better than that do I have to do?" This will pin the buyer down to a specific.

3. Concentrate on the dollar amount that's being negotiated. Don't be distracted by the gross amount of the sale and start thinking percentages.

4. A negotiated dollar is a bottom-line dollar. Be aware of what your time's worth on an hourly basis.

5. You'll never make money faster than you will when you're power negotiating.

Never Offer to Split the Difference

The next rule is that you should *never offer to split the difference when you're negotiating.* In this country, we have a tremendous sense of fair play. It dictates that if both sides give equally, then that's fair. By which I mean that if Fred puts his home up for sale at $200,000 and Susan makes an offer at $190,000, and both Fred and Susan are eager to compromise, both of them tend to think, "If we settled at $195,000, that would be fair, because we've both given equally."

Maybe it's fair; maybe it isn't. It depends on the opening negotiating positions that Fred and Susan took. If the house is really worth $190,000 and Fred was only holding to his overinflated price to take advantage of Susan's having fallen in love with his house, then it's not fair. If the house is worth $200,000 and Susan is willing to pay that but she's taking advantage of Fred's financial problems, that isn't fair either.

Don't fall into the trap of thinking that splitting the difference is the fair thing to do when you can't resolve a difference in price with the buyer. They offer $75,000. You've been negotiating for a while, during which time you've been able to get the owners of the property up to $80,000, and you've come down to $84,000 with your proposal. Where do you go from there? You have a strong feeling that if you offered to split the difference, they would agree to do so, which would mean agreeing at $82,000.

Instead of offering to split the difference, here's what you should do. You should say, "Well, I guess this is just not going to fly. It seems like such a shame, though, when we've both spent so much time working on this proposal." People become more flexible in relationship to how long they've been negotiating. "We've spent so much time on this proposal and we've come close to a price with which we could both live. It seems like a shame that it's all going to collapse when we're only $4,000 apart."

If you keep stressing the time you've spent on it and the small amount of money that you're apart on the price, eventually the other people will say, "Look, why don't we split the difference?"

You act dumb and say, "Let's see, split the difference. What would that be? I'm at $84,000. You are at

$80,000. You're telling me you'd come up to $82,000. Is that what I hear you saying?"

In doing this, you have immediately shifted the negotiating range from $80,000–$84,000 to $82,000–$84,000, and you have yet to concede an additional dime.

So you say, "$82,000 sounds a lot better than $80,000. Tell you what: let me take it to my partners." (I'll teach you in a later chapter why you should always have a higher authority you have to check with.) "I'll tell them that you came out to $82,000 and we'll see if we can put it together. I'll get back to you tomorrow."

The next day, you can get back to them and say, "Wow, my partners are tough to deal with right now. I felt sure that I could get them to go along with $82,000, but we spent two hours last night going over the figures again, and they insist that we'll lose money if we go a penny below $84,000. Golly, we're only $2,000 apart on this job now. We're not going to let it all fall apart when we're only $2,000 apart."

If you keep that up long enough, eventually they'll offer to split the difference again. If you are able to do that, this gambit has made you an extra $1,000 of bottom-line profit.

Even if you can't get the other party to split the difference again and you end up at the same $82,000 that you would have done if you had initially offered to split the difference, something very significant has happened here: they think they've won because you got them to propose splitting the difference at $82,000: you've gotten your partners to reluctantly agree to a proposal that the other party made. If you had suggested splitting the difference, you would have been forcing them to agree to a proposal that *you* had made. That may seem like a very subtle thing to you, but it can dramatically affect who has felt they won and who has felt they lost.

Remember, the essence of power negotiating is to always leave the other side thinking that they won. So the rule is, never offer to split the difference, but always encourage the other person to offer to split the difference.

The counter-gambit when the buyer tries to get you to split the difference is to use higher authority: "It seems reasonable to me, but I don't have the authority. If you propose it, I'll take it to my people and I'll see if I can get them to accept it."

Key points to remember about not offering to split the difference

1. Don't fall into the trap of thinking that splitting the difference is the fair thing to do.
2. Splitting the difference doesn't mean down the middle, because you can do it more than once.
3. Never offer to split the difference. Instead, encourage the other side to offer to split the difference.
4. By getting the other party to offer to split the difference, you have put them in a position of suggesting the compromise. Then you can reluctantly agree to their proposal, making them feel that they won.

The Hot Potato

The *hot potato* is when the buyer wants to give you their problem and make it your problem.

What hot potatoes do your buyers toss you? Do you ever hear, "We just don't have it in the budget"? Whose problem is it that they didn't budget properly for your fine product or service? It's their problem, not yours, but they'd like to toss it to you and make it yours.

Another hot potato is, "I can't authorize that." Again, whose problem is that? The other party hasn't developed the trust of the people they report to. It's their problem, yours, but they'd like to toss it to you and make it yours.

You've probably had a customer call you to say, "I need you to move my delivery up. If those parts are not here first thing in the morning, the entire assembly line comes to a screeching halt."

Whose scheduling problem is that? It's his, right? Not yours. But he'd liked to give you his problem and make it yours.

From my study of international negotiations, I've found out that exactly the same principles apply the same rules that apply for the negotiators in Geneva doing nuclear control talks apply to you when the other side is putting pressure on you. The same things apply, and the same responses are appropriate.

Here's how the international negotiators would tell you to respond to the hot potato: test it for validity right away. This is what international negotiators do: when

....
The *hot potato*: When the buyer wants to give
you their problem, and make it your problem.
....

the other side tries to give them their problem, they test it for validity right away. You have to find out right away whether it really is a deal killer that the other party has tossed you or simply something that they've thrown on to the negotiating table to judge your response. You must jump on it right away. Later on, it's too late. If you continue to work on their problem, soon they believe that now it's your problem, and it's too late to test it for validity.

My background is as a real estate broker. I used to be president of a twenty-eight-office company in Southern California. In real estate, we used to get tossed hot potatoes all the time. The buyer would come into one of our offices and say, "We only have $10,000 to put down." Even in blue-collar areas, that would be a very low down payment. Our real estate agent might work with it, but it would be tough.

I would teach the agents to test for validity right away: tell the buyers, "Maybe we can work with $10,000, but let me ask you this: Say I find exactly the right property for you in exactly the right neighborhood. The price and terms are fantastic. Your family is going to love it, your kids are going to love having their friends over to play, but it takes $15,000 to get in.

Is there any point in showing it to you, or should I just show it to my other buyers?"

Once in a great while, the person would respond, "Don't you speak English? $10,000 is it, and not a penny more. I don't care how good a buy it is." But nine out of ten times, they would say, "We really didn't want to touch our certificate of deposit, but if it's a really good buy, we might. Or maybe Uncle Joe would help us with the down payment." Immediately the agent found out that the problem the buyer tossed her was not the deal killer that it had appeared to be.

If you sell home furnishings, one of your customers might say, "We've got $20 a yard for carpeting, and that's it." If you catch that hot potato instead of tossing it back, you will probably start thinking of cutting prices right away, because you've assumed that what they told you was final. Instead, test for validity up front by saying, "If I could show you a carpet that would give you double the wear, still be looking good five years from now, and cost you only 10 percent more, you'd want to take a look at it, wouldn't you?" Nine times out of ten, they'll say, "Sure, we'll take a look at it," and you immediately know that price is not the deal buster that it appeared to be.

Another way to counter the hot potato of "We don't have it in the budget" is to simply say, "Who *does* have the authority to exceed the budget?"

Sometimes you'll kick yourself at what happens next. They'll say, "It would take a vice president to authorize that."

So you say, "Well, you want to do it, don't you? Why don't you call the vice president and see if you can get an OK to exceed the budget? Fair enough?" And the customer will pick up the phone to call the vice president and argue for an OK.

Sometimes it's that simple, but in any event, you have to test for validity right away. I remember doing a seminar in Alaska. They had put me up at the Anchorage Hilton, and on my day of departure I needed a late checkout. Two clerks were standing right next to each other behind the registration desk, and I said to one of them, "Would you give me a six o'clock checkout in my room, please?"

"Mr. Dawson, we could do that for you, but of course we'd have to charge for an extra half day."

"Who would have the authority to waive that charge?"

The clerk pointed to the person standing right next to her and said, "She would."

So I leaned over and said to the other clerk, "How would you feel about that?"

She said, "Oh, sure. That would be fine. Go ahead."

Another way to handle the hot potato of "We don't have it in the budget" is to ask them when their budget year ends.

I trained eighty salespeople at one of the top health maintenance organizations in California. A few weeks before the meeting, the training director called me and suggested that we have dinner together so that she could fill me in on how the company operates. Since I figured that she was going to pay for dinner, I picked the top French restaurant in Orange County, and we had a great dinner.

As we were having dessert, I said, "You know what you should do? You should invest in a set of my cassette tapes for each of your salespeople so that they have the advantage of a continuing learning process." As I said that, I was mentally computing that eighty salespeople at $65 per set of tapes would be another $5,200 in income on top of the speaking fee (to which they'd already agreed).

The training director thought about it and said, "Roger, that would probably be a good idea, but we just don't have it in the budget."

I need to make a confession here. I'm very ashamed of what I thought next, but I want to share it with you because it may help you if you've ever had the same shameful thought: "I wonder if she would say yes if I cut the price." Isn't that a shameful thought? She hadn't said a thing about the tapes costing too much. She hadn't told me that she might be tempted if I lowered my price. She had simply told me that she didn't have it in the budget.

Fortunately, I caught myself in time, and instead I did what I teach, which is to test for validity. I asked, "When does your budget year end?" This was August, and I thought that she would tell me December 31.

To my surprise, she said, "At the end of September."

"So you would have it in the budget on October 1?"

"Well, yes, I suppose that we would."

"Then no problem. I'll ship you the tapes and bill you on October 1. Fair enough?"

"That would be fine," she told me in less than thirty seconds.

I made a $5,200 sale because I knew that when the training director tossed me her problem, I should test for validity.

Look out for people giving you their problems. You have enough of your own, don't you?

It's like the businessman who was pacing the floor at night. He couldn't sleep, and his wife was also getting frantic. "Darling, what's bothering you? Why don't you come to bed?"

"We have this huge loan payment due tomorrow, and the bank manager's a good friend of ours. I hate to face him and say that we're not going to have the money to pay him."

So his wife picked up the phone and called their friend the bank manager, and said, "That loan payment we have coming due tomorrow—we don't have the money to pay it."

The husband exploded. He said, "What did you do that for? That's what I was afraid of."

The wife said, "Well, dear, now it's his problem, and you can come to bed."

Don't let other people give you their problems.

In short, the counter-gambit to the hot potato is to test for validity right away by asking, who has the authority to exceed the budget, or who has the authority to waive that charge? Or when does your budget year end? If you can break through the barrier of the problems they're trying to give you (even if they are hypothetical), you have eliminated the hot potato.

In our next chapter, I'll teach you why the value of the service you perform always seems to go downhill. Then I'll teach you a technique that a vice president at a Fortune 50 company told me was the most important thing he'd ever learned at a seminar. I'll also teach you how to nibble and how to stop the buyer from nibbling on you.

In this chapter, you've learned these techniques:

- Vise Technique: *"You'll have to do better than that."*
- Vise Countergambit: *"Exactly how much better than that do I have to do?"*
- You should never "split the difference."
- Don't let a buyer give you his/her problem.

Chapter Four

Nibbling and the Value of Services

I n this chapter, I'll teach you three more key principles: First, why the value of the service you perform always seems to go downhill. Then I'll teach you a technique that a vice president at a Fortune 50 company told me was the most important thing he'd ever learned at a seminar. I'll also teach you how to nibble and how to stop the buyer nibbling on you.

The Declining Value of Services

First, let me tell you about the principle of the declining value of services. It teaches you something that you can count on in dealing with buyers: any concession you make to them will quickly lose its value. The value of any material object you buy may go up in value over the years, but the value of services always appears to decline rapidly after you have performed those services.

For this reason, power negotiators know that anytime you make a concession to the buyer in a negotiation, you should ask for a reciprocal concession right away, because the favor that you have done the buyer now loses value very quickly. Two hours from now, the value of it will have diminished substantially.

Real estate salespeople are very familiar with the principle of the declining value of services. The seller of a property has a problem: they need to sell the property. The real estate salesperson offers to solve that problem for a 6 percent listing fee. At that point, it doesn't sound like an enormous amount of money, but the minute that the realtor has performed the service by finding the buyer, then suddenly that 6 percent starts to sound like a tremendous amount of money. Say the property sells at $200,000: 6 percent is $24,000. The seller is saying, "For what? What did the realtor do? All she did was put it in the multiple listing service." Actually, she did much more than that by marketing the property and negotiating the contract. But remember the principle: the value of a service always appears to diminish rapidly once you have performed that service.

I'm sure that you've experienced that. A buyer with whom you do a small amount of business has called you. They're in a state of panic because the supplier from whom they get the bulk of their business has let them down on a shipment. Their entire assembly line has to shut down tomorrow unless you can work miracles and get a shipment to them first thing in the morning.

So you work all day and through the night, rescheduling shipments all over the place, against all odds. You're able to get a shipment there just in time for the assembly line to keep operating. You even show up at the buyer's plant and personally supervise the unloading of the shipment.

The buyer loves you for it. He comes down to the dock where you are triumphantly wiping the dirt off your hands and says, "I can't believe you were able to do that for me. This is unbelievable service. You are absolutely incredible. Love you, love you, love you."

So you say, "Happy to do it for you, Joe. That's the kind of service we can give when we have to. Don't you think it's time we looked at my company being your sole supplier?"

He replies, "That does sound good, but I don't have time to talk about it now, because I've got to get over to the assembly line to be sure that it's running smoothly. Come to my office Monday morning at ten o'clock and we'll go over it. Better yet, come by at noon, and I'll buy you lunch. I really appreciate what you did for me. You are fantastic."

All weekend long, you think, "Boy, do I have this one made!"

But Monday rolls around, and negotiating with the buyer is just as hard as ever. What went wrong? The declining value of services came into play.

Again, the value of a service always appears to decline rapidly after you have performed the service. This tells you that *if you make a concession during a negotiation, get a reciprocal concession right away*. Don't wait. Don't sit there, thinking that because you did them a favor, they owe you and they will make it up to you later. With all the goodwill in the world, the value of what you did goes down rapidly in their mind.

For the same reason, consultants know that they should always negotiate their fee up front, not afterward. Plumbers know that. They know that the time to negotiate with you is before they do the work, not after. I had a plumber out to the house. After looking at the problem, he slowly shook his head and said, "Mr. Dawson, I know what the problem is, and I can fix it for you. It'll cost you $150."

"Fine," I said. "Go ahead."

It took five minutes to do the work.

"Now wait a minute," I said. "You're going to charge me $150 for five minutes' work? I'm a nationally known speaker, and I don't make that kind of money."

Key points to remember about the declining value of services

1. The value of a material object may go up over time, but the value of services always appears to go down.
2. Don't make a concession trusting that the other side will make it up to you later.
3. If you sell your services, negotiate your fee before you do the work.

"I didn't make that kind of money either when I was a nationally known speaker," he replied.

The Trade-off Gambit

Now let's talk about a gambit that will probably make you thousands—maybe tens of thousands—of dollars a year once you start using it. The *trade-off gambit* tells you that any time the buyer asks you for a concession in the negotiations, you should automatically ask for something in return.

Let's say that you sell forklifts and you've sold a large order to a warehouse-style hardware store. They've requested delivery on August 15, thirty days ahead of their grand opening. Then the operations manager for the chain calls you and says, "We're running ahead of schedule on the store construction. We're thinking of moving up the opening to take in the Labor Day weekend. Is there any way you could move up the delivery of those forklifts to next Wednesday?"

You may be thinking, "That's great. They're sitting in our local warehouse ready to go, so I'd much rather move up the shipment and get paid sooner. We'll deliver them tomorrow if you want them."

Even though your initial inclination is to say, "That's fine," I still want you to use the trade-off gambit. I want you to say, "Quite frankly, I don't know whether we can get them there that soon. I'll have to check with my scheduling people" (note the use of a vague higher authority) "and see what they say about it. But let me ask you this. If we can do that for you, what can you do for us?"

One or all of three things is going to happen:

1. **You might just get something**. They may have been thinking, "Boy, we've got a problem here. What can we give them as an incentive to get them to move this shipment up?" So they may just concede something to you. They may say, "I'll tell accounting to cut the check for you today," or "Take care of this for me, and I'll use you again for the store that we're opening in Chicago in December."

2. **By asking for something in return, you've elevated the value of the concession**. When you're negotiating, why just give a thing away? Always make a big deal out of it. You may need that later on. Later on, you may need to go to them and say, "Do you remember last August, when you needed me to move that shipment up for you? You know how hard I had to talk to my people to get them to reschedule all our shipments? We did that for you, so don't make me wait for our money. Cut me the check today, won't you?" When you elevate the value of the concession, you set it up for a trade-off later on.

3. **It stops the grinding away process**. This is the key reason you should always use the trade-off gambit. If they know that every time they ask you for something, you are going to ask for something in return, it stops them from constantly coming back for more.

....
The *trade-off gambit*: Any time the buyer asks
you for a concession in the negotiations, you
should automatically ask for something in return.
....

I can't tell you how many times a salesperson has come up to me and said, "Roger, can you help me with this? We thought we had a sweetheart of a deal put together. We didn't think that we would have any problems at all with this one, but in the early stages, they asked us for a very small concession. We were so happy to have the business that we told them, 'Sure, we can do that.' A week later, they called us for another small concession, and we said, 'All right, I guess we can do that too.' Ever since then, it's been one darn thing after another. Now it looks like the whole thing is going to fall apart on us."

They should have known up front that when the other side asked them for that first small concession, they should have asked for something in return: "If we can do that for you, what can you do for us?"

I trained the top fifty salespeople out of a Fortune 50 company that manufactures office equipment. They have what they call their key account division, which negotiates their largest account with the biggest customers. These people are heavy hitters. There was a salesperson at the seminar who just made a $43 million sale to an aircraft manufacturer—and that's not a record. When I trained people at a huge computer manufacturer's training headquarters, I had a salesperson in the audience who had just closed a $3 billion sale, and he was in my seminar taking notes. This key account division had its own vice president, and he came out to me afterward to tell me, "Roger, that thing you told us about trading up was the most valuable lesson I've ever learned in any seminar. I've been coming to seminars like this for years and I thought that I'd heard it all, but I've never been taught what a mistake it is to make a concession without asking for something in return. That's going to save us hundreds of thousands of dollars in the future."

Jack Wilson, a Chicago television producer, told me that soon after I taught him this gambit, he used it to save several thousand dollars. A television studio called and told him that one of the camera operators was sick. Would Jack mind if they called one of the camera operators that Jack had on a contract and asked him if he could fill in? It was really just a courtesy call—something to which Jack would have said, "No problem" in the past. However, this time he said, "If I do that for you, what will you do for me?" To his surprise, they said, "Tell you what. The next time you use our studio, if you run into overtime, we'll waive the overtime charge." They had just conceded several thousand dollars to Jack on something that he never would have asked for in the past.

Please use these gambits word for word the way that I'm teaching them to you. If you change even a word, it can dramatically change the effect. If, for example, you

Key points to remember about the trade-off gambit

1. When asked for a small concession by the other side, always ask for something in return.

2. Use this expression, exactly as it is worded: "If we can do that for you, what can you do for us?" Don't change the wording and ask for something specific in return, because it's too confrontational.

3. You may just get something in return.

4. It elevates the value of the concession so that you can use it as a trade-off later on.

5. Most importantly, it stops the grinding away process.

change this from, "If we can do that for you, what can you do for us?" to, "If we do that for you, you will have to do this for us," you have become confrontational at a very sensitive point in the negotiations: when the other side is under pressure and is asking you for a favor. Of course, you're tempted to take advantage of this situation and ask for something specific in return. Don't do it. It could cause a negotiation to blow up in your face when you ask what they will give you in return. They may say, "Not a darn thing," or "You get to keep our business. That's what you get." That's fine, because you had everything to gain by asking and you haven't lost anything. If necessary, you can always revert to the position of insisting on a trade-off by saying, "I don't think I can get my people to agree to that unless you are prepared to accept a charge for expedited shipping or you're willing to move up the payment date."

Nibbling

Now let's talk about nibbling. It's an important gambit, because it accomplishes two things. First, it enables you to sweeten the deal you've made with the buyer, and second, you can use it to get the buyer to agree to things that he wouldn't agree to earlier.

Car salespeople understand this, don't they? They know that when they get you onto the lot, there's a psychological resistance that is built up to the purchase. They know to first get you to the point where you're thinking, "Yes, I'm going to buy a car. Yes, I'm going to buy it here." Even if it means closing you on any make and model of car, even a stripped-down model that carries little profit for them, they can get you into the closing room and start adding on all the other little extras that really build the profit into the car.

The principle of nibbling tells you that you can accomplish some things more easily with a nibble later on in the negotiations. Children are brilliant nibblers, aren't they? If you have a teenage child living at home, you know that they don't have to take any courses on power negotiating. They're naturally brilliant negotiators—not because they learn it in school, but because when they're little, everything they get, they get with negotiating skills.

When my daughter Julia graduated from high school, she wanted to get a really great graduation gift for me. She had three things on her hidden agenda. First, she wanted a five-week trip to Europe. Second, she wanted

....

The *nibble gambit*: Asking for extra amounts
or concessions later on in the negotiation.

....

$1,200 in spending money. Third, she wanted a new set of luggage. She was smart enough not to ask for everything up front. She was a good enough negotiator to first close me on the trip. Then she came back a few weeks later and showed me in writing (because people are more likely to believe what they see in writing) that the recommended amount of spending money was $1,200; she got me to commit to that. Then right at the last minute, she came to me and said, "Dad, you wouldn't want me go to Europe with a raggedy set of luggage, would you? All the kids will be there with new luggage," and she got that too. Had she asked for everything up front, I would have negotiated out the luggage and negotiated down the spending money.

What's happening here is that a buyer's mind always works to reinforce decisions that it has just made. Power negotiators know how this works and use it to add that little extra profit to the job that can make the difference between profit and loss.

Why is nibbling such an effective technique? To find out why this works so well, a couple of psychologists did a study at a racetrack in Canada. They studied the attitudes of people immediately before they placed a bet and again immediately after. They found out that before bettors placed a bet, they were very unsure and anxious about what they were going to do. But once they had made the decision to place the bet, suddenly they felt very good about what they had just done and often wanted to double the bet before the race started. In essence, their minds did a flip-flop. Before they made the decision, they were fighting it; once they'd made the decision, they supported it.

If you're a gambler, you've had that sensation, haven't you? Watch them at the roulette tables in Atlantic City or Las Vegas. The gamblers place their bets; the croupier spins the ball. At the very last moment, people are pushing out additional bets. The mind always works to reinforce decisions that it has made.

Once I spoke at a Philadelphia convention when the Pennsylvania lottery prize was $50 million. Many of the people in the audience were holding tickets. To illustrate this principle, I tried to buy a lottery ticket from somebody in the audience. Do you think they would sell me one? No, they wouldn't—even for fifty times the purchase price. I'm sure that before they brought that ticket, they were unsure and anxious about betting money on a 100 million to one shot. However, having made the decision, they refused to change their minds. The mind works to reinforce decisions that it has made earlier.

So one rule for power negotiators is, *don't necessarily ask for everything up front.* You wait for a moment of agreement in the negotiations and then go back and nibble for a little extra. You might think of the power negotiating process as pushing a ball uphill. This ball is much bigger than you, and you're straining to force it up to the top of the hill. The top of the hill is the moment of first agreement in the negotiations. Once you reach that point, then the ball moves easily down the other side of the hill. This is because people feel good after they've made the initial agreement. They feel relief that the tension and stress is over. Their mind is working to reinforce the decision that they've just made, and they're more receptive to additional suggestions you may have.

The Second Effort

After the buyer has agreed to make any kind of purchase from you, it's time for the second effort. Football coach Vince Lombardi always used to talk about the second effort: Football receivers almost caught the ball, but it slipped through their fingers. But instead of giving up, they made the second effort. They dove and caught the ball before it hit the ground. He was also proud of film clips of the running back who is almost brought down, but still wiggles free and makes the touchdown.

Vince Lombardi used to say that everybody makes the first effort. You wouldn't be on the team if you didn't know how to play the game well and weren't doing everything that coaching experts tell you do when you're on the field. But everybody's doing that. The players on the other team are doing that. The players who would like to replace you on the team are capable of doing that. The great ones always make the second effort. Just doing everything their coach expects to do isn't good enough for them.

You wouldn't be selling for your company unless you knew how to play the selling game well, and you were out there doing everything that your company expects you to do. However, everybody's doing that. The people who sell for your competition are doing that. The people who apply for your job every day in the personnel office are capable of doing that. The difference between a good salesperson and a great salesperson is that the great ones always make another effort. Even when they know their sales manager would pat them on the back and tell them not to feel bad because they did everything they could to get the sale, that's not good enough for the superstar. They always make another effort. So always go back at the end for that second effort.

Perhaps you sell packaging equipment, and you're trying to convince your customer that they should go with the top-of-the-line model, but they're balking at that kind of expense. You back off. But after you've reached agreement on all the other points, you come back and nibble for it before you leave. You say, "Could we take another look at the top-of-the-line model? I don't recommend it for everyone, but with your account of volume and growth potential, I really think it's the way for you to go. All it means is an additional investment of $500 a month." You have a good chance of their saying to you, "All right, if you think it's that important, let's go ahead."

Perhaps you sell office equipment, and part of your program is an additional investment for an extended service contract. But when you present it, the buyer says, "We're not interested in service warranties. We realize how much profit you make on them, and we're in a good cash flow position. When the equipment needs servicing, we'll pay for it."

At that point, you may be thinking that you're not going to risk the sale for the sake of the service warranty, so you back off. Before you leave, have the courage to say, "Could we take another look at that extended service warranty? You may be missing the preventive maintenance factor: your employees will call us much sooner if they know that the contract covers the cost of the call, and our technicians can spot trouble before it starts. Your equipment will last longer because you've made this investment. I really think it's the way for you to go, and all it means is an additional investment of $45 a month." You have a good chance that they will say, "All right, if you think it's that important, let's go ahead." Always go back at the end to make a second effort for something that you couldn't get the other party to agree to earlier.

On the other hand, look out for people nibbling on you. There's a point in the negotiation where you are very vulnerable, and that point is when you think the negotiations are all over.

I bet you've been the victim of a nibble at one time or another. You've been selling a car to someone, and you're finally feeling good because the buyer pressure and the tension of the negotiations have drained away. They buyer is sitting in your office writing out the check. Just as they're about to sign their name, they look up and they say, "That does include a full tank of gas, doesn't it?"

You are at your most vulnerable point in the negotiations here for two reasons. First, you've just the sale and you're feeling good. When you feel good, you tend to give things away that you otherwise wouldn't. Second, you're thinking, "Oh no, I thought we'd resolved everything. I don't want to take a chance on going back to the beginning and renegotiating the whole thing. If I do that, I might lose the entire sale. Perhaps I'm just better off giving in on this little point." So you are most vulnerable just after the buyer has made the decision to go ahead.

Look out for buyers nibbling on you. You've made a huge sale and are so excited that you can't wait to call your sales manager and tell him what you've done. The buyer tells you that he needs to call purchasing and get a purchase order number for you while he's on the phone. He puts his hand over the mouthpiece and says, "Oh, by the way, you can't give us sixty days on this, can't you? All of your competitors will."

Look out for people nibbling on you because you've just made a big sale and you're afraid to reopen the negotiations for fear of losing it. You'll have to fight the tendency to make the concession.

Try to keep a buyer from nibbling on you, first by showing them in writing what any additional concessions will cost them. List extended terms (if you ever make them available), but show them what it costs to do that. List the cost of training, installation, extended warranties, and anything else for which they might nibble. Second, don't give yourself the authority to make any concessions.

Protect yourself with higher authority and the good guy/bad guy gambit that I'll teach you in chapter 10.

The counter-gambit to the nibble is to gently make the buyer feel cheap. You must be careful about the way you do this, because you're at a sensitive point in the negotiation. You smile sweetly and say, "Oh, come on. You negotiated a fantastic price with me. Don't make us wait for our money too. Fair enough?" That's the counter-gambit of the nibble when it's used on you. Be sure that you do it with a big grin on your face so they don't take it too seriously.

So now that you've learned the fine art of nibbling, always consider these points as you go into negotiations:

1. There are some elements that you're better off to bring up as a nibble after you've reached initial agreement.

2. Do you have a plan to make a second effort on anything to which you couldn't get them agree the first time around? Power negotiators always take into account the possibility of being able to nibble. Timing is very critical. Catch the other person when the tension is off and they feel good because they think the negotiations are all over. On the other hand, look out for the buyer nibbling on you at the last minute, when you are

feeling good. At that point, you're the most vulnerable and liable to make a concession; half an hour later, you'll be thinking, "Why on earth did I do that? I didn't have to do that. We'd agreed on everything already."

Here are the key points to remember about nibbling.

1. With a well-timed nibble, you can get things at the end of the negotiation that the other party wouldn't agree to earlier.

2. This approach works because the buyer's mind reverses itself after it has made a decision. At the start of the negotiation, they may have been fighting the thought of buying from you, but after they've made a decision, you can nibble for a bigger order, an upgraded product, or additional services.

3. Willingness to make that additional effort is what separates great salespeople from merely good salespeople.

4. Stop the buyer from nibbling on you by showing them in writing the cost of any additional features, services, or extended terms, and by not revealing that you have the authority to make any concessions.

5. When the buyer nibbles on you, respond by making them feel cheap in a good-natured way.

6. Avoid post-negotiation nibbling by addressing and tying up all the details and using gambits that cause the other party to feel that they've won.

★　★　★

The next chapter will be a change of pace, because I'm going to move away from negotiating gambits and talk about how to control the buyer instead of letting them control you.

Three principles you have learned in this chapter:

1. Why the value of the service you perform always seems to go downhill.

2. The trade-off gambit always asks for something in return when the buyer asks you for a small concession.

3. How to nibble at the end of the negotiation and how to stop the buyer from nibbling on you.

Chapter Five

The Elements of Power

Personal power always affects the outcome of the sale. Whenever you are in front of a buyer, you develop a feeling about how much power you have over him or her. Sometimes it's a mild feeling of confidence that you can make the sale. You may be thinking, "I feel lucky today." Sometimes it's a much stronger feeling: you feel that you have all the power, assured that you can make the sale without making any concessions.

Perhaps this is an objective feeling: you feel confident because you know that the buyer needs what you have. More often in sales, it's subjective: you feel it, but you don't know why.

In this chapter, I'm going to demystify that feeling. At the end, you'll understand where your personal power comes from. You'll also understand what buyers are doing when they seem able to intimidate you.

Legitimate Power

The first element of personal power is *legitimate power*. Legitimate power goes to anybody who has a title, because titles influence people. If the title on your business card says, *vice president*, you already have a head start over someone whose card says, *salesperson*. When I ran a real estate company, I would let the agents who were farming a territory put *area manager* on their business cards. Farming means that they'd staked out an area of 500 homes, and they were knocking on doors and mailing newsletters to those homeowners to establish themselves as experts in those communities. They told me that having the title of area manager on their cards made a dramatic difference to the way people accepted them. If you have a title, use it on your business card, your letterhead, and your nameplate, because titles do influence people.

Legitimate power also tells you that you should have the other party come to you if possible rather than negotiating on their territory, where they are surrounded by their trappings of power. If you are taking the other party somewhere, it should always be in your car, because it gives you more control. If you're taking them to lunch, it should be to your choice of restaurant, not to their favorite place, where they feel in control.

Use your title, but don't be intimidated because the person to whom you're selling has a fancy title: some of these titles don't mean a thing. My daughter, Julia, graduated from the University of Southern California with a degree in business finance and went to work for Dean Witter, the New York stockbroker, in their huge Beverly Hills office. One day she was talking about becoming a vice president. I told her, "Julia, you must set realistic goals in life. That's a huge corporation, and it may take you years and years to become a vice president." She replied, "Oh, no, I think I'll be a vice president by the end of the year."

"How many vice presidents does Dean Witter have?" I asked.

"I don't know, but it must be thousands. We have thirty-five in this one office."

That company understood that titles influence people, so don't be intimidated if the person to whom you're selling has a fancy title, because it may not mean a thing.

There are other forms of legitimate power positioning. In the marketplace, if you can claim that your company is the biggest or the smallest, the oldest or the newest, you have legitimate power. You can claim to be the most global company, or you can claim to specialize. You can tell the buyer that you're brand-new, so you're trying harder, or that you've been in the business for forty years. It really doesn't matter how you position yourself. Any kind of positioning gives you legitimate power.

Reward Power

The second element of personal power is *reward power*. Power negotiators understand that any time you perceive someone can give you a reward, you have given them the power to intimidate you. If you think that buyer is rewarding you by giving you an order, you've given them the power to intimidate you. Therefore you feel more intimidated when you're making a big sale than you do when you're making a small sale. The potential reward is greater, so you feel intimidated.

Say you can claim to be the best in the business: they can't do any better than you. If you are willing to put your personal reputation and expertise, and your company's, on the line to solve that buyer's problems, they are not rewarding you; you are rewarding them.

Of course, you can't push that too far, because it quickly becomes arrogance, but don't roll over the other way, thinking that the buyer would be rewarding you by giving you an order. I've heard rumors that some salespeople will beg a buyer to give them just a small part of their business. Can you believe that? Doesn't it sound like a dog begging for table scraps? When you truly believe that you are rewarding the buyer, not the other way around, you'll feel confident in demanding all of their business.

When the buyer starts using reward power on you, recognize it, and don't let it intimidate you. Some buyers are absolute masters at using reward power. They're asking you for a concession, and they just happen to mention that they have a big job coming online next week for which you might be in the running. Or they'll talk about their yacht down at the harbor or their ski cabin up in the mountains. They don't even have to come out and tell you that if you did business together, you'd get to use those things. It's just implied reward power. Don't let it irritate you, but recognize it for what it is, and don't let it throw you off base in the negotiations. Once you recognize reward power and understand what they're trying to do to you, the other party's ability to control you with it goes away, and you become a lot more self-confident as a negotiator.

Coercive Power

The opposite side of that coin is *coercive power*. Any time you perceive that someone is able to punish you, they have power over you. You know how awful you feel when the state trooper pulls you over to the side of the road, and he's standing there and can write you a ticket or not. The penalty may not be very great, but the level of intimidation is very great indeed.

Any time you perceive someone is able to punish you, they have the power to intimidate you, and one of the strongest punishments we know is the power to embarrass people.

Any time you perceive that someone else is able to punish you, they have power over you.

In chapter 1, I told you that you should make your initial proposal so high that it brackets your real objective. Sometimes that's intimidating: you simply don't have the courage to make those way-out proposals because you are afraid the other side will laugh at you. The fear of ridicule stops you from accomplishing many things with your life, and you need to come to grips with it.

As with reward power, the answer lies in experience. While a new salesperson may fear losing a $1,000 sale, the experienced salesperson will not let the loss of a $100,000 sale intimidate them.

New salespeople always have trouble with reward and coercive power. When they first make sales calls, they see every buyer as being able to reward them by giving them the order or punish them by turning them down, or worse yet, ridiculing them for what they have proposed. Once they've been at it for a while and recognize that selling is a numbers game, just like anything else, if they're working hard at it and talking to a great number of people, there always will be a high percentage of people who will turn them down. Once they understand that, their perception that people can reward or punish them goes away, and they become a lot more self-confident in what they're doing.

Reverence Power

The fourth element of power is *reverence power*. It goes to anybody who has a consistent set of values. An obvious example of this would be a religious leader, like the pope, Billy Graham, or the late evangelist Robert Schuller. John F. Kennedy had reverence power. When he talked about the New Frontier, he was projecting that he believed in something, that he had a consistent set of values. His brother, Robert, was very good at it too when he ran for president. If you want to influence people, you must project a consistent set of values.

Lack of reverence power was President Carter's downfall. He was one of the most moral and ethical presidents we've ever had. He was also one of the hardest-working men who ever occupied the White House, and probably among the most intelligent: he majored in nuclear physics. However, he lost his ability to influence because he appeared to vacillate on different issues. We never knew if he felt strongly enough about his position to follow through if the going got tough.

You like and admire consistent behavior in your customers; they like and admire it in you. If you are willing to take a stand for your principles—especially if it appears that you're risking financial loss—it builds trust in the other person, and they love you for it. For example, you might sell computers and have the courage to say to your customers, "Of course you'd like to save money, and I'd favor it too if it were the right thing for you to do, but it isn't. I know that you won't be completely happy unless you get the model with the 500-gigabyte hard drive, so I'm sorry; I won't sell you anything less." They'll love you for that. Of course, it'll raise a few eyebrows, but if you've done your homework and if you are right, you'll have power with that customer. If you back down, how are they going to respect you?

Suppose that you have the misfortune to have a heart attack.

You wake up in a hospital bed, and a doctor is telling you that you need triple bypass heart surgery. You say, "I think I can get by with a double bypass." If he says, "OK, let's try a double bypass and see how it works out," how would you feel about him? Would you let him near you with a scalpel? I don't think so.

When you project reverence power, buyers notice it. They admire and respect a consistent set of values, and it gives you influence over them. When you're negotiating with a buyer and you indicate a willingness to cut corners or in some way pull some strings that you shouldn't be pulling, you may get a short-term gain in your ability to make that sale. However, you get a long-term loss in your ability to influence that buyer over a long period of time.

Be careful that you're not setting up your standards and then breaking them. Don't tell that buyer that you would never cut prices and then go ahead and do it. That's worse than not setting up the standards in the first place.

Charismatic Power

The fifth element of personal power is *charismatic power*. I'm sure you've had the experience of meeting a celebrity who has an overwhelmingly charismatic personality.

When I met President Bill Clinton, I was uncomfortable because I'm at the opposite end of the political spectrum from him, and I'm sure he could sense that I didn't want to say anything that would constitute an endorsement, so I said, "Good luck, Mr. President; don't let them get you down."

He looked me straight in the eye, read my name badge, and said, "Roger, if you'll stay with me, I'll be there."

"I'll be there, Mr. President," I said.

Within fifteen seconds, he'd gotten a commitment of support from me strictly based on the power of his personality.

Salespeople tend to overemphasize charismatic power. Many a salesperson has told me, "The only reason my people do business with me is because they like me." Not nowadays. Don't fall into the Willy Loman trap. Even in the 1940s, when Arthur Miller wrote *Death of a Salesman* and had his protagonist, Willy Loman, saying, "The most important thing is to be liked," Miller was making fun of the idea. Sure, that buyer is more likely to give you an order if he or she likes you, but don't think that it gives you much control. Buyers are much too sophisticated for that today. It's a long way from control of the negotiations.

. . . .

Salespeople must not fall into the
"Willy Loman Trap": Being "liked" will not
necessarily get you the sale.

. . . .

Expertise Power

Next is *expertise power*. When you project to people that you have more expertise than they do in a particular area, you develop power over them. Attorneys and doctors really play this one up. They develop a whole new language that you can't understand in order to project to you that they have an expertise that you don't have. There's not a reason in the world why doctors couldn't write prescriptions in English, but if they did, it would take away a little of that mystique, a little of that expertise power. Attorneys are the same way; they develop a whole new language that we can't understand so that they can project expertise power.

Don't let buyers intimidate you with expertise power. Remember when you first started in sales and you studied up on the technical side of what you sold, but you weren't confident about it yet? Then you ran into a buyer who appeared to know more about it than you. Remember how intimidating that was? Don't let the buyer do it to you.

When the buyer questions your expertise, don't be afraid to say, "Well, that's not my area of expertise, but our engineers are the finest in the business; you can have complete confidence in them."

Combining the Three

Now let's take a look at these last three together: reverence power, charismatic power, and expertise power.

Power negotiators know that these three are critical if you are to control the negotiations.

Do you know someone who doesn't seem to have half the problems that you have when they're selling? Perhaps you've been out on a call with your sales manager, and she made it look so easy. She sat down with the buyer and chatted with him for fifteen or twenty minutes. She didn't appear to be talking about anything of consequence, but at the end of that time, the buyer was saying to her, "What do we have to do here? Do we need to go with the top of the line, or can we get by with the standard? You tell us; you're the expert."

Here's how your sales manager got that much power over the buyer: she did a good job of projecting reverence power, charismatic power, and expertise power. Reverence power: "I won't do anything that is not in your best interest, regardless of the gain to me." That builds trust, doesn't it? Charismatic power: she has a likable personality. Expertise power: without becoming overbearing, she projected to the buyer that she knew more about the product than he did. When you put those three together, you're very close to control of the negotiations; you're very close to the point where the buyer will defer the decision. He'll say, "What do you think we should do?" He has surrendered control of the negotiation to you.

Situation Power

The seventh element of personal power is *situation power*. I'm sure that you've been the victim of situation power. This is the person down at the post office: normally very powerless in any other area of life, but in this particular situation, they can accept or reject your package. They have power over you, and don't they love to use it! Situation power is prevalent in large organizations or government agencies, where the people don't have much latitude in the way they perform their jobs. When they do get some latitude, when they have some power over you, they're eager to use it.

Sometimes you get to the point where people have so much situation power over you that you're going to lose this one, regardless of how good a negotiator you are. If you have to make the concession anyway, regardless of what you do, you might as well make it as gracefully as you can. It doesn't make any sense to get so upset about it that you lose the goodwill of the other person, even though you still must make the concession.

But how many times have we been into a department store to get a refund and the clerk says, "All right, we'll do it this one time, but it's not our normal policy." What sense does that make? If you have to make a concession anyway, you might as well make it gracefully so that you maintain the goodwill of the other person.

Don't let situation power upset you. Power negotiators know it for what it is. Pass on and move into an area where you do have some control.

Information Power

The final element of personal power is *information power*. Sharing information forms a bond. Withholding information tends to intimidate. Large companies are skillful about doing this.

They'll develop a level of information at the executive level that they won't share with the workers. It's not because the information is that secretive or it would do any harm to disclose it. It's because these large corporations know that a level of secrecy at the executive level gives them control over the workers.

Humans have a tremendous desire to know what's going on. We can't stand a mystery. You can put a cow in a field, and it'll stay in that field all its life and never wonder what's on the other side of that hill. Human beings will spend billions of dollars to throw a Hubble telescope out into space because we have to know what's going on out there.

Withholding information can be very intimidating. You've made an extensive presentation to a buying committee, and they say to you, "We need to talk about this for a moment. Would you mind waiting outside in the lobby? We'll call you when we're ready for you." Is it any wonder that you feel uncomfortable sitting outside in the lobby? We hate it when people withhold information from us. They may be just doing this as a negotiating gambit: they may be in there talking about football scores, for all we know. But when we walk back into the negotiations, our level of power has gone down and theirs has gone up. The moment we realize what they may be doing, they can no longer intimidate us with that gambit.

The Eight Elements of Power

The eight elements that give you power over the buyer are: Legitimate power, Reward power, Coercive power, Reverence power, Charismatic power, Expertise power, Situation power, and Information power.

When you get a chance, rate yourself in regard to each of these elements—not as you see yourself, or maybe not even as you really are, but as you think other people see you. How do your buyers perceive you in each of these eight areas? (Rate *reward power* and *coercive power* separately.) Give yourself a score from 1 to 10 in each of these areas, 1 being very weak and 10 being very strong.

Add the scores up, which gives you a potential score of 80. If your score comes out in the 60s, that's a very good number for a power negotiator: you have power, but you still have empathy for the other side. If your score is over 70, I'd be concerned that you'd be too intimidating in dealing with people. Less than 60, and you have some weak spots. Examine those elements where you gave yourself a low rating, and see what you can do to get yourself up to a 10.

As you review this list, remember that these eight elements are also ways the buyer can intimidate you

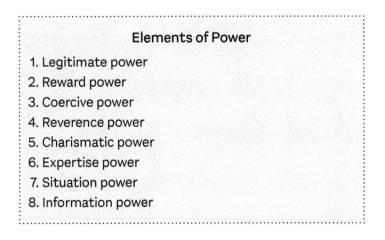

Elements of Power

1. Legitimate power
2. Reward power
3. Coercive power
4. Reverence power
5. Charismatic power
6. Expertise power
7. Situation power
8. Information power

into thinking that you don't have any power. The next time you are negotiating and you feel that you've lost control and that they're beginning to intimidate you, identify which of these elements is getting to you. Identifying it will help you handle it.

The Four Critical Areas

Pay particular attention to the four critical ones for power negotiators: *legitimate power*, the power of the title; *reward power*, the ability to reward people; *reverence power*, a consistent set of values; and *charismatic power*: personality, pizazz.

The effects of these four together are cataclysmic. When they come together in one person, what happens is incredible. This is how Adolf Hitler got control of Germany in the 1930s. He kept stressing the title: "Führer, Führer, Führer." He kept stressing reward

> The four most critical types of power for Power Nego-
> tiators:
>
> 1. Legitimate Power
> 2. Reward Power
> 3. Reverence Power
> 4. Charismatic Power

power: he kept saying to the German people, "If we invade Czechoslovakia and Poland, this is what we'll get." He had reverence power—"We'll never deviate from this"—and he had a hypnotic charismatic power. He could hold tens of thousands of people mesmerized with his oratory. These are the trademark of all cult leaders.

On the good side, it's when you get a John F. Kennedy. Every president has the power, the title; every president is able to reward, but not every president is able to project a consistent set of values. That was the albatross of both Jimmy Carter and Bill Clinton: they appeared to vacillate. It was Richard Nixon's undoing; he was also dogged by the fact that few people liked him.

Not every president is able to project charismatic power. This was Gerald Ford's problem. He had the other three elements in great abundance, but he didn't have the personality with which to put power across throughout his career. I think it was George H.W. Bush's downfall also, particularly since he followed Ronald Reagan, who was so charismatic. John F. Kennedy and Ronald Reagan both had these four qualities in great abundance, and it put them among the most popular presidents in modern history.

You can have that kind of power over your buyers if you concentrate on developing those four elements of personal power. When you do, I promise you that you'll see a remarkable transformation in your ability to control your buyers.

In this chapter, I've taught you how to use your personal power to control the buyer instead of letting them control you. I've taught you the things that the buyer can do to you to cause you to blink first in the negotiation, and the things that you can do to take control of the sales process.

You'll be fascinated with the next chapter, because I'm going to teach you how to analyze your personality style and the personality style of your buyers. Then I'll teach you how to adapt your negotiating style to the personality style of the buyer.

Chapter Six

Understanding Personality Styles

I n this chapter, I'm going to teach you how to analyze your personality style and the personality style of your buyers. Then I'll teach you how to adapt your negotiating style to the personality style of the buyer to whom you're selling.

The system I'm going to teach you is based on something that the ancient Greeks worked out centuries ago, so it is time-tested and proven. Nonetheless, it may contradict much of the sales training that you've received.

I'm sure you've been to one of those training classes that teach you canned responses to any objection the buyer might raise. But power negotiators know that you have to adapt your approach to the personality styles of different buyers.

Assertiveness Levels

This system is based on two dimensions. The first dimension is the *assertiveness level* of the buyer. You tell this by such details as the firmness of the handshake, how easily they volunteered their name when they shook hands with you, and the directness of their responses to your questions.

The assertive buyer wants to get down to business quickly. He or she will shake hands and say, "Come on in, and let's see what you have for me." An assertive buyer will quickly make a decision: "I'll take a truckload if you'll give me 20 percent discount off of list. Have them here by the fifteenth, and take care of the freight. Do you want the deal or not?"

Assertive people are always eager to sell their ideas and philosophies to other people, so they are typically persuaders. They also have short attention spans: their minds are constantly jumping from one thing to another. They're thinking of all the phone calls they must make and all the things they have to do, because they know they won't be thinking about the same thing five minutes from now. They have the habit of making decisions quickly. They'll look at your proposal and either go for it or not go for it quickly.

By contrast, less assertive people want to take time to get to know you; they also want time to think over a decision or refer it to a committee. They have long attention spans, so they get in the habit of making decisions slowly. They genuinely need time to think things over.

Power negotiators recognize this as a major point of conflict in closing the sale. If you're a fast decision maker, the less assertive decision makers drive you up the wall. You'll be thinking, "He's had that proposal for a week now; I will call him up, and he'll say he's still thinking about it. How long does it take anybody to make up their mind? It's only $200,000. It's not that big a deal."

If you're an unassertive person, you're probably a slow decision maker, and you're very suspicious of fast decision makers. You say, "I took the proposal in to the buyer, and she looked at it briefly—it couldn't have been more than three or four minutes—and said, 'Fine, let's go with it.' That company must have the worst credit rating in the world. There's no way we'll ever get paid. It's just not natural for people to make decisions that quickly."

Emotional Levels

The second dimension is the *emotional level* of the buyer. This is the same as the left-brain versus right-brain way of thinking: emotionally right-brain people are creative and care about *people*, whereas emotionally left-brain people care about *things* and see them in black-and-white. Evaluate the way the buyer talks about things and the warmth with which he or she responds to people.

Personality Styles

	Assertive	Unassertive
Emotional	Extravert	Amiable
Unemotional	Pragmatic	Analytical

THE PRAGMATIC

If you combine the assertiveness and emotional dimensions, you come up with four different styles. First is the *assertive unemotional* person, who might be called a *pragmatic*. The pragmatic buyer will typically have his call screened. His secretary will want to know who is calling and what you're calling about before putting the call through. The business environment will be formal. He'll have a secretary who places his calls and confirms appointments for him and who will usher you into the office rather than the buyer coming out of his office to meet you.

Pragmatics like participation sports such as skiing, scuba, diving, and flying. They may like golf but hates how long it takes, and typically won't take the time to play. They're tidy, highly organized, and always dress formally.

With the pragmatic, don't waste time with small talk. You are there to make a proposal, not chitchat. Their eyes will glaze over if you try to build rapport by

> With the pragmatic, don't waste time with small talk or overload them with information—they'll make decisions with the least amount of information necessary.

talking about the basketball game last night. Don't overload pragmatics with information. They'll make decisions with the least amount of information necessary. If you try to sway them with an excessively enthusiastic presentation, you'll come across as a phony. Expect a fast decision, based strictly on facts.

THE EXTRAVERT

Second is the *assertive emotional* person, whom I call the *extravert*. Extravert buyers are friendly and open. They'll place they own telephone calls and don't necessarily want their incoming calls screened. If you go to their place of business, they will tend to meet you in the lobby and give you a personal tour of the company.

They greet everybody warmly as they walk around the building.

Extraverts love the excitement of spectator sports such as baseball or football. They'll probably have family pictures in their office—something a pragmatic thinks is too informal. They like to spend time talking about their vacations. If somebody comes into the office for a business decision or if they take a call while you're there, they'll make the decision quickly.

Extraverts are warm and friendly, but they're not afraid to say no to you. They're personable, but at the same time they're assertive. They're not particularly organized, and their desks are usually cluttered. Although they have poor follow-up, they're likable and fun to be with.

When you're dealing with extraverts, paint an enthusiastic picture of the benefits to them. Get them excited. Talk about their interests, which probably include football and baseball. Get to them by telling stories of triumph and disaster. Expect a fast decision based on their level of excitement about the project.

THE AMIABLE

Third is the *unassertive emotional* person, whom I call the *amiable*. Amiables tend to set up barriers. They probably have unlisted home phone numbers and may have a "No Peddlers" sign on their front doors. They tend to live in the same home for a long time, because they develop relationships with things as well as with people. They often drive older cars because they fear going down to the dealer and getting ground to death by a high-pressure salesperson.

Amiables are not entrepreneurs. They prefer managing in a large corporation, where the format of the organization protects them from having to make assertive decisions. They seem to have a poor sense of time management: call and ask for an appointment, and they'll tell you to drop by any time. They tend to be disorganized, because they can't say no to people.

When asked to be on a committee, they have a tough time refusing, so they tend to take on more work than they can handle. Their environments are warm and comfortable, because they form relationships with the things in their lives, such as homes, furniture and cars, and don't like to change them.

When you're dealing with an amiable, go slowly. Wait until they trust you; demonstrate that you really care about people. Be careful, because the slightest little thing will offend this person. Don't high-pressure them, because they don't like being forced into decisions. You'll just have to acknowledge that and give them time to think things through, because you have to wait until they feel comfortable with you.

THE ANALYTICAL

The fourth personality style is the *unassertive unemotional* person, whom I call the *analytical*. The analytical will most likely have an engineering or accounting background. They often have a gadget mania and are surrounded by computers and other high-tech devices.

Analyticals are very curious: they soak up information and can't get enough. Show them a book, and they'll want to know when and how it was printed. In a management situation, analyticals think they can manage everything just by generating massive amounts of information.

Analyticals are very precise about punctuality, so you'll never hear them saying, "I'll be there around lunchtime." They would say, "I'll be there at 12:15 p.m."

They're also very precise about figures. They won't tell you that something costs just over $100; they'll tell you that it costs $104.16. If you ask them what day of the week it is, they'll tell you it's Wednesday, except on the island of Tonga, where it's already Thursday morning. They love precision so much that when you tell them the specifications of your product, carry it out to two decimal places. With the analytical, be accurate.

As their name suggests, analyticals are fascinated by analysis and have charts and graphs for everything.

Quick summary of the Four Personality Styles

- **The Pragmatic**: The *assertive unemotional* person, formal business environment, likes sports, highly organized, makes fast decisions with least amount of information necessary.
- **The Extravert**: The *assertive emotional* person, warm and friendly, personable but assertive, not particularly organized, poor follow-up, fast decision-maker based on level of excitement.
- **The Amiable**: The *unassertive emotional* person, tend to set up barriers, generally not entrepreneurs, tend to be disorganized with poor time management skills, prefer status quo and resist change, prefer a slow approach with no high-pressure.
- **The Analytical**: The *unassertive unemotional* person, usually an engineering or accounting background, love high-tech gadgets, very curious and very punctual, fascinated by charts and graphs, like to drill down into the details.

When they ask you for figures, give them to the penny. Be prepared to provide every little detail of the operation. Build rapport by talking about their interests, which probably include engineering and computer technology.

Myths of Sales Training

Once you realize how easy it is to identify the personality style of the buyer, you'll find yourself questioning many of the things you have been taught in sales training.

For example, you were taught to always be enthusiastic, weren't you? How can you expect the buyer to be enthusiastic about your product or service if you are not? Enthusiasm is wonderful with the extravert, because they'll feed off that kind of excitement, and it's also great with the amiable, because they'll a warm feeling from the enthusiasm: "You can just sense how good he feels about that, so it must be a good idea."

By contrast, pragmatics are turned off by enthusiasm: "Oh, don't give me that phony sales pitch. Just give me the facts I need to decide." Similarly, there's no way you can tell me that analyticals will be bowled over by enthusiasm. They won't decide until they feel they have enough information.

Another thing that I'm sure you learned in sales training is to dominate the conversation. When someone asks you a question, answer with another question: "Can you deliver it in thirty days for me?" "Would you like it delivered in thirty days?" "Does it come in blue?" "Would you like it in blue?" "Can you give me ninety days to pay?" "Would you like ninety days to pay?"

This is great with analyticals, because they love questions; they'll sit there all day asking and answering questions. It's also great with amiables, because it's a sign that you care about them.

But when pragmatics ask you a question, they want answers. They don't want to play verbal ping-pong with you. It's the same with extraverts. They won't warm to you unless you deal with them in a straightforward and open manner. They'll make a fast decision, but it will be based on facts.

Another thing that you've probably been taught is that people buy with emotion, not logic; the only reason they need any logic at all is to justify the emotional decision they've just made. That's true with the extravert personality. It's also true with the amiable, because the emotion translates into a warm feeling about you and what you do. But pragmatics don't spend money with emotion; they spend because it's going to generate the return they want. Analyticals don't make a buying decision with emotion either. They'll make a buying decision when they feel that all the numbers are in line.

Dealing with Opposite Styles

You will have the most difficulty with the personality style who is different from you in both the assertive and emotional dimensions. If you are an assertive unemotional—a pragmatic—you love other pragmatics. They're down-to-earth, no-nonsense people, and if you ask them a question, you'll get an answer. When you want a decision, you'll get it.

But if you are an assertive who is dealing with the unassertive, emotional amiable, you'll run into difficulty, because you are thinking quickly and emotionally while they're thinking slowly and emotionally. You'll make a proposal to an amiable and not see a reason in the world why they shouldn't go along with it: clearly you can provide a better product at a lower price than their present vendor, so they ought to dump that vendor and go with you. But they hold back. They're thinking, "I don't feel comfortable with you yet. I want to do business with people around whom I feel comfortable. Don't tell me how much you know until you tell me how much you care."

Conversely, the amiable will have the most difficulty with pragmatics such as you. You seem so hardheaded and impersonal to them. You seem to be all business, with no feeling for people, so the amiable doesn't feel good about doing business with you.

. . . .

If you are an assertive, who is dealing with the unassertive, emotional amiable, you'll run into difficulty, because you are thinking quickly and emotionally while they're thinking slowly and emotionally.

. . . .

If you are an assertive, emotional extravert, you love other extraverts. They're fun people who will go off and do exciting things at the drop of a hat. But when you have to deal with the unassertive, unemotional analytical, you run into difficulties. To you, analyticals always seem to need too much information. They're too much into the details and don't seem to be able to see the big picture. To you, they're far too cautious in the way they do things, because to an analytical, accuracy is next to godliness. When an analytical says to you, "When will you deliver the shipment?" he doesn't want to hear you say, "Oh, about the middle of January or so." He wants to hear you say, "January 16, at 3:15 in the afternoon." He wants to hear it out to the minute. When he says, "What's the thickness of paint you'll use on the casing?" he doesn't want to hear, "All medium." He wants to hear it down to a thousandth of an inch.

Conversely, the analytical thinks that you as an extravert are too flippant. You're too easygoing. You go off on different tangents without really knowing all the information that you want to know about the situation.

Personality Styles in Negotiation

Now let's talk about how each of these personality styles negotiate differently.

In a negotiating situation, the pragmatic turns into a street fighter. A street fighter is a person whose only goal in the negotiation is to win, and to them, winning means that somebody else has to lose. "What's wrong

> Don't talk win-win to a street fighter.
> Instead, bleed all over him and tell him
> how much you are hurting.

with that? That's the way the world is. Don't waste my time with all this wishy-washy, win-win nonsense. Why on earth would I be concerned about the other party's needs in the negotiations? I expect them to fight as hard for what they want as I'm going to fight for what I want."

You would think that the street fighter would be the one you'd least like to see sitting behind a buyer's desk, but they have a vulnerable flaw: they become obsessed with one issue in the negotiation, because they see negotiating as a game to be won or lost, and they must have a way to score the game. So the street fighter buyer may decide that winning the negotiation with you means getting you down to a lower price than their present supplier. They will become obsessed with that one issue.

But if you realize this, you'll find that they'll give away everything else in order to attain that goal. Let's say that you sell commercial real estate and you have a street fighter seller who has made up his mind that he won't take a penny less than $10 million for his shopping center. If you take him an offer at $9.8 million, he'll turn it down, because he would feel that he was losing. However, if you took him an offer at $10 million and asked him to carry back a $1 million straight note with 6 percent interest added, due and payable in ten years—which is a worse offer than the $9.8 million cash out offer, if you consider the time value of money—he will accept it, because it meets the criteria by which he's scoring the game.

Another thing about street fighters is that in order for them to feel that they've won, they must see that somebody else is losing. Don't talk win-win to a street fighter. Instead, bleed all over him and tell him how much you're hurting.

As a negotiator, the extravert turns into a den mother: someone who gets so excited about things that they tend to lose perspective. This is the person in your office who's organizing a softball team, and they're so excited and enthusiastic about it that it doesn't occur to them that there's anybody in the entire world who doesn't want to play softball on Tuesday night. Den mothers are the people most likely to have the whole negotiation fall down around them without realizing there was a problem. You'll see them come back into the office and kick the desk: "How can they do this to me? I was out drinking with them until midnight the other night."

As a negotiator, the amiable tends to turn into a pacifier. Their objective is not so much to win as to see that everybody is happy. It's interesting to see the opposite personality style, the street fighter, negotiating with the pacifier, because the street fighter will grind every last dime out of the negotiations, convinced there's not another penny left on the table. When it's all over, the pacifier will turn to them and say, "Now, are you sure this is fair? I wouldn't want to take advantage of you."

The analytical tends to turn into an executive style negotiator. Typically, the analytical buyer is an engineer or an accountant, so everything's OK as long as it's been buttoned down, nailed down, and in its place. Analyticals don't like the push and shove of negotiating. They like everything to be rigid and in its place. Their favorite expression is, "It's the principle of the thing."

The opposite personality style, the extravert den mother, will say, "Hey, look, we're talking $500 here, so for heaven's sake, let's split the difference and get the thing going."

The analytical, executive style negotiator will reply, "I understand that we're talking $500. Since you're proposing we split it, we're only talking $250, aren't we? At this point, it's the principle of the thing I'm concerned about." If you're an analytical, be careful that you're not too rigid in the way that you negotiate.

The Power Negotiator Difference

Now let's look at these different personality styles and see how their style of negotiating differs from what I want you to become, which is a power negotiator. Let's look at each element of the negotiations.

First, let's look at goals in negotiations. The pragmatic street fighter's goal is clear. His goal is victory. He wants to win in the negotiations. The extravert den mother's goal is to influence the other people. He has so much fun changing other people's minds that he loves to take a position against the other side just to see if he can turn their thinking around. The amiable pacifier's goal is agreement. He feels that if he can get everybody to agree on something, everything else will fall into place. The analytical executive's goal is to have order in the negotiations, to get the negotiation on a formal format, so that the procedures established produce a solution.

But the goal of the power negotiator is a wise outcome for all parties involved. Let's look at the relationships that exist in the negotiating process when you have these different personality styles involved.

Street fighters tend to scare people. They're sitting on the edge of hostility, implying, "If you don't go along with what I want, it's going to get very uncomfortable here, and you are not going to like it." The den mother personality tries to do it all by inspiring the other person: getting them so excited that they'll be able to sway them. Pacifiers want to develop relationships: "If we like each other well enough, we'll all agree" is their philosophy. The executive ignores relationships and negotiates strictly based on facts.

The power negotiator learns how to separate the people from the problem by bringing them back from their emotional relationships with each other and concentrating on the resolution of the issue.

Now let's look at the negotiating style of each of the four. The style of the street fighter is hard and domineering. The style of the den mother is excitable. The style of pacifiers is soft, maybe too soft: they may too easily give in on things. The executive remains detached from the personalities.

Power negotiators learn how to be soft on the people, but hard on the problem. They're easygoing, friendly, likable, and courteous with all the people involved in the negotiations, but he keeps hammering away and concentrates on the problems.

Each of the four personality styles has its own fault in negotiation. The street fighter, the dominant personality, tends to dig into a particular position, determined to get what she wants from the negotiation. She won't budge even if it would be better to yield. The den mother tends to ignore the others and isn't sensitive enough to what's really going on in the negotiations. The pacifier's fault is he's too easily swayed, and the executive's fault is that she's inflexible.

Their methods of negotiating differ greatly. Street fighters demand losses from the other people: they don't feel they can win unless others lose. The den mother wants to inspire people and turn them on to a particular idea, feeling that if they're excited about it enough, they'll go for it. Pacifiers tend to accept losses. Their theory is that if they make concessions, the other side will want to reciprocate. Executives tend to be too rigid in their style of negotiating.

The power negotiator, however, learns how to create options in the negotiations where nobody loses. The power negotiator works to get people off the positions that they have taken (largely because of their personality styles) so that they can concentrate on interests. This is a key point, because positions can be 180 degrees apart, whereas interests can be identical.

Look at the changing relationship between the United States and the Soviet Union during the Cold War. For forty years, the Soviets had adopted the position that there's no sense arguing with the capitalists: they're not going to change until they dominate the world; why negotiate with them? Similarly, we Americans had taken the position that the Russians were so inflexible that it was a waste of time to talk to them. We knew that they wouldn't stop until they had dominated the world with their philosophy.

Those were positions that both sides took. For forty years, they concentrated on positions. But positions can be 180 degrees apart even when interests are identical. Without question, both nations had a mutual interest in world peace. They both had an interest in reducing military expenditures. They both had an interest in becoming trading partners.

A power negotiator learns to get people off positions that they have taken so they can concentrate on mutual interests. The key is to become familiar with the different personality styles of your buyers and learn how they approach things differently. Then, even though they may have taken a radically different position from yours, work on getting them off that position and concentrating on your mutual interests.

End of chapter reminder

When it comes to personality styles:

- First, identify whether the person is assertive or not.
- Second, identify whether the person is emotional or not.

In this chapter, I've taught you how to analyze your personality style and the personality style of your buyers. Then I taught you how to adapt your negotiating style to the personality style of the buyer to whom you're selling. Analyzing the personality style of your buyers is powerful stuff, but you have to work at it. If you do, it will only be a week or two before you're quickly able to place your buyers on the personality quadrant. From that, you'll understand their negotiating their style and adapt your style to match theirs. Remember to first analyze whether the person is assertive or not, and then determine if they're emotional or not.

The next chapter will be a lot of fun, because we're going to talk about something that's becoming very important in our rapidly changing business environment: how to negotiate with foreigners and people of different ethnic backgrounds.

Chapter Seven

Negotiating with Foreigners

I'm an immigrant: I came here from England when I was twenty-two. I'm very conscious of the enormous ethnic diversity in this great country, so even if you don't sell directly to foreign buyers, the chances are good that it won't be long before you will.

In the first part of this chapter, I'll discuss how to negotiate with foreigners, since Americans negotiate in a very different way from other nationalities. Then, in the second half, I'll teach you how to analyze the force that's driving the other side in a negotiation. Knowing that is the key to win-win negotiation.

Just about everybody has had a frustrating experience dealing either with a foreigner in a foreign country or with a person of foreign origin who lives in this country. Although I've been here for decades, I can relate to the difficulty of dealing with foreigners as well as of adapting to the American way of doing things. I've also traveled to ninety-four other countries around the world. Because of my background, it's easy for me to see why foreigners misunderstand us. I know how different America is from any other country on earth and how America is deceptively different for foreigners. They think they know us from watching our movies and television shows. But movies and television shows don't always reveal what is in the American heart and mind, and that is what determines our approach to business.

Conversely, we tend to look at foreigners and think we understand them. True, they may dress in Western business suits and speak our language, but that doesn't mean that their traditional values and mindsets have changed. They may prefer American music and movies, but their beliefs in their way of life and the values they place on their traditions are as strong as ever.

I believe that underneath all our apparent similarities, there are enormous differences in our approach to business. So let's unravel the mysteries of negotiating with foreigners.

We Americans live in a very deal-conscious environment. Sociologists might tell you that this is because we're such a mobile and diverse society that we have

....

Underneath all of our apparent similarities, there
are enormous differences between Americans'
and foreigners' approach to business.

....

little sense of roots. Instead of trusting people and the
way things are done, as is common around the world,
we place all of our trust in creating an unbreakable
deal: will it hold up in court? We act as though anyone
who doesn't consider the possibility of having to defend
the deal in court is naive.

Yet most foreigners reject our dependence on the
deal. Should they choose to sign a contract at all, it is
simply an expression of an understanding that existed
between the parties on a particular date; it is a formal
expression of a relationship that now exists between the
parties. As with any other relationship, it must mold
itself to changing conditions.

It astounds most Americans to learn that you can
sign a contract in South Korea and have it mean nothing six months later. "But we signed a contract," the
American complains.

"Yes," their Korean counterpart patiently explains.
"We signed a contract based on the conditions that
existed six months ago, when we signed it. Those conditions no longer exist, so the contract we signed is
meaningless."

"Foul!" cries the American. "You're trying to
cheat me!"

Not at all. What seems to be disreputable action to us is not so to them, and we should not interpret it that way. It is merely their way of doing things.

It often delights Americans who are selling to people from the Middle East that they have had so little trouble getting a contract signed. Then they are horrified to find out that in the Arab world, signing a contract announces the *start* of the negotiations, not the end. A signed contract means less in their culture than a letter of intent does in ours.

I'm not putting this down, and you shouldn't either. Instead, you should recognize that different nationalities and cultures have different ways of doing things. If you plan to sell to them, it behooves you to learn, understand, and appreciate those ways.

It won't surprise you to learn that Americans resort to legal action more quickly and frequently than any other people on earth. This would be laughable to a salesperson in many countries, where the civil legal system is close to nonexistent. Before you put too much dependence on that contract you signed with a foreign buyer, perhaps you should figure out how you could enforce adherence to it. Even if you're selling in a country that does have an operative legal system for civil lawsuits, the damage it could do you might mean it's not worth pursuing.

In America, legal action is so common that companies continue to do business with a company that is suing them. We see it as a normal way to resolve a dispute and no reason for rancor. In most foreign countries, there is such a loss of face involved in being sued that they will refuse to deal with you in any way once you've sued them.

In addition to concentrating more on the deal than on the relationship between the parties, the other major mistake that we Americans make in dealing with foreigners is that we want to get down to business too quickly. Nobody gets down to business faster than Americans do. Typically, we exchange a few pleasantries to ease any tension and then get right down to hammering out the details of the deal; we socialize afterwards. Foreigners may take days, weeks, or even months before they feel comfortable moving from the getting to know you stage to the point where they feel good about doing business with you.

When the Shah of Iran fell from power, the real estate company that I ran in Southern California did a huge amount of business with Iranians who were fleeing the new regime, often with millions in cash to invest. Often I would watch our people make the mistake of trying to talk business too soon, which caused the Iranians to distrust them. Quickly we learned that they needed time to size us up. They wanted to sit and drink tea for several hours before talking business.

If you fly to Japan, you may have to socialize for many days before they feel that it's appropriate to talk business. Be careful that they're not just trying to push you up against a time deadline. Many people have told me that their joy at being treated so well soon turned sour as they realized how difficult it would be to get down to business at all. They have told me horror stories of not being able to negotiate until they were in the limousine on the way back to the airport. True. It's a two-hour ride out to Narita airport, but that's negotiating under excessive time pressure. Terrified at the thought of going home empty-handed, they went straight to their bottom line.

In short, you are likely to fall into two major traps when selling to foreigners: you will overemphasize the deal without attaching enough importance to the relationship of the parties, and you'll get down to business too quickly. (The two are closely related, of course.)

Building a relationship with a foreign buyer to the point where you feel comfortable with them takes time. Enlarging on that relationship to the point where you trust them and they trust you, so that you don't have to rely on the contract being airtight, takes a great deal of time.

Two major traps when selling to foreigners:

1. Overemphasizing the deal, without putting enough emphasis on the relationship between the parties.
2. Getting "down to business" too quickly.

The Typical American

Let's look at some of the major characteristics of the typical American businessperson. Of course, this may not describe you accurately, but if you identify with any of these characteristics, you should adapt your approach when selling to foreigners.

1. **To foreigners, you will probably seem very direct in your communications**. You use expressions such as "What's your bottom line?" or "How much profit would you make at that figure?" Or you try to shift the emphasis of the negotiations by saying, "Let's lay our cards on the table," or "Let's wrap this one up tonight." While this kind of directness puts pressure on the other side, foreigners may see it as too blunt, which will probably offend them.

2. **Because you're an American, you probably resist making outrageous initial demands**. This goes back to your hope that you can cut the deal and get out of Dodge. Because you want to blitz the negotiations and wrap them up quickly, you tend to think in much shorter time frames than do foreigners. You're thinking you can conclude the negotiations in hours, while they're thinking it will take many days. Thus they may make outrageous initial demands, knowing that the price and terms will change enormously as days go by. You see that as slowing the negotiations down by drawing you both into endless haggling.

3. **You are more likely to negotiate alone than foreigners are**. It's not unusual to find a lone American negotiator showing up at an international negotiation fully empowered to do business and find a team of ten or twelve negotiators from the other side. (You may be able to put together a team of three if it includes your interpreter and driver.) Of

course, this is not good for you, because you'll feel psychologically overwhelmed unless the negotiating teams are roughly the same size. Even so, the effect on the foreign team concerns me more: they may interpret a lone negotiator as meaning that your company is not serious about making a deal at this meeting. They may conclude that this must only be a preliminary expedition or that you're merely gathering information to take back to your team. Unless you understand this fact and take pains to explain that you are the entire negotiating team and that you are empowered (at least up to a point) to negotiate the deal, they may not take you seriously.

4. **You are probably uncomfortable with emotional displays**. The English are the worst, of course, but Americans also see displaying emotions in public as a weakness. If an American's wife starts to cry, for example, he will probably assume that he has done something devastatingly cruel to her. In the Mediterranean countries, the husband would simply wonder what ploy his wife had concocted. If you fear an emotional reaction, you'll be tentative in your sales to foreigners, and if the buyer does explode with anger at one of your proposals, you tend to overreact. Instead, you should merely see it as a negotiating ploy that might be perfectly acceptable in their culture.

5. **You tend to expect short-term profits**: Besides wanting to conclude the negotiations before you build

a relationship with the other side, you also expect quick results from the deal that you cut. Realize that you look at quarterly dividends, whereas foreign investors are looking at ten-year plans. Our outlook comes across—unfairly, I think— as a fast-buck mentality, while they're looking to build a long-term relationship with us. You appear to concentrate only on profits, and this can be offensive to them.

6. **You are less likely to speak a foreign language**. There's no question that English is becoming the business language of the world. Conferences in Europe are typically conducted in English these days, because it is the common denominator language. Most European businesspeople can speak two foreign languages, and one of them is always English. Most Asian businesspeople can at least understand English even if they cannot speak it well. Sadly, hardly any Americans can speak German or Japanese. If you do know a foreign language, it's probably Spanish or French.

   To realize how arrogant this may appear to foreigners, you only must think of how frustrated you became when you first dined in a Parisian restaurant when the waiter didn't appear to speak any English. You probably thought (as I did) that this is a tourist restaurant; they must get English-speaking people in here all the time. Why is he being so difficult by refusing to speak English?

Unfortunately, this attitude is all too prevalent with American businesspeople. Our expectation that if they want to do business with us, they should learn our language can come across as irritatingly arrogant to a foreigner. Instead, you should always appear surprised and delighted that they can speak even a few words of our language. You should always try to speak a few words of their language, even if it's only to say good morning and thank you.

7. **You're probably uncomfortable with silence**. Fifteen seconds of silence seems like an eternity to you. But particularly to Asians, who are comfortable with long periods of meditation, this impatience appears to be a weakness that they can exploit. When dealing with foreigners, don't be intimidated by long periods of silence. Instead, see it as a challenge to not be the next one to talk.

   After an extended period of silence, the next person to talk loses: the next person to open their mouth will make a concession.

8. **You hate to admit that you don't know** (a subject I'll discuss more in the next chapter). Again, this is something that foreigners know and can use to their advantage. You don't have to answer every question. You're perfectly entitled to say, "That's privileged information at this stage," or simply tell them that you don't know or are not permitted to release the information they seek. Not every question deserves an answer.

9. **If they've given you a gift, you probably feel obligated**. You will often be overwhelmed with hospitality and gifts by the foreigners with whom you'll be negotiating. This is an overt attempt to win your favor, and you must deal with it. Rather than giving offense by refusing their favors, the best plan is to reciprocate, which eliminates any personal obligation that may have been created. If they take you out to dinner, you should take them to an equally expensive place. It eliminates the obligation, and you have twice the fun.

Finally, permit me to do a little flag waving here: people around the world still admire and respect Americans, particularly American businesspeople. They trust us and see us as straightforward in our business dealings, so please don't feel that I've been pointing out the shortcomings of Americans when we deal with foreigners. I've been teaching you only how Americans are misperceived by foreign negotiators. Fair enough.

After an extended period of silence, the next person to talk loses: The next person to open their mouth will make a concession.

Negotiating Drives

Many different things may be driving a buyer when they're negotiating with you, although you probably don't think much about it. You tend to assume that what drives the buyer is the same thing that drives you, (which is getting the best deal). Sociologists call this *sociocentrism*, meaning that you tend to feel that the buyer wants what you would want if you were them.

Power negotiators know that what we would want if we were the buyer may have nothing to do with what they really want. Power negotiators know that the better we can understand what is driving the buyer—what the buyer really wants to accomplish—the better we can fulfill the buyer's needs without taking away from our position.

Poor negotiators get into trouble because they fear that they will be vulnerable to the buyer's tricks if they let the buyer know too much about them. Instead of wanting to find out what is driving the buyer by revealing his own drives to the buyer, the poor negotiator lets his fears stop him from being that open.

Let's look at the different things that drive buyers when they're negotiating with you. Recognizing and understanding these drives is a major key to win-win negotiating.

The *competitive drive* is the one that salespeople know best, and it's why they see negotiating as being so challenging. If you assume that the buyer is out to beat you by any means within the rules of the game, of course you'll fear meeting a buyer who might be a better negotiator or more ruthless than you.

The competitive drive exists at many used-car lots. The used-car dealer attracts customers by offering the

....

Power Negotiators must avoid *sociocentrism*—
meaning that you tend to feel that the buyer
wants what you would want if you were them.

....

lowest prices in town but pays its salespeople based on
the amount of profit they can build into the sale. It's
a gladiatorial approach to negotiating. The customer
wants to buy for the lowest price, even if the dealer loses
money and the salesperson loses their commission.
The salesperson wants to drive the price up because
that's the only way they can make any money. Sound
the trumpets, let the spectacle begin, and may the best
person win.

Competitive drive negotiators believe that you
should find out all you can about the buyer but let the
buyer know nothing about you. Knowledge is power,
so competitive drive negotiators believe that the more
you find out and the less you reveal, the better off
you'll be. When gathering information, the competitive drive negotiator distrusts anything the buyer might
say, because it may be a trick. They gather information covertly by approaching the other employees at the
buyer's company. Since they assume that the buyer is
doing the same to them, they work assiduously to prevent the leaking of information from their side.

This approach assumes that there has to be a winner and a loser. What's missing is the possibility that
both sides could win because they're not out for the

same thing, and the fact that by knowing more about the buyer, you can concede issues that are important to them but may not be significant to you.

The *solutional drive* is the best negotiating situation and the one we all enjoy. This is when the buyer is eager to find a solution and is willing to calmly discuss with you the best way to do that. It means that both sides will negotiate in good faith to find a win–win solution.

Solutional negotiators tend to be wide open to creative approaches, because they feel that there must be a better solution out there somewhere that hasn't occurred to them yet. It takes an open mind to be creative. The great thing about negotiating with someone with a solutional drive is that they have written nothing in stone. They're not restricted by company policy or tradition. They feel that everything is negotiable, because everything was at one time negotiated. Short of breaking the law or their personal principles, they will listen to any suggestion you care to propose, because they do not see you as in competition with them.

It sounds like the perfect solution, doesn't it? Here you have both sides cooperating to find the fair and perfect solution. But there is one caveat. The buyer could be feigning when they appear to be in the solutional drive. Once you put your cards on the table and told them exactly what you're prepared to do, they may revert to competitive negotiating. So if it seems too good to be true, be wary.

Next is the *personal drive*. You may encounter situations where the buyer's main drive is neither to win for winning's sake nor to find the perfect solution: their main drive is their personal profit or aggrandizement. A case that quickly comes to mind is that of an attorney who is working on a fee basis rather than a contingency basis. The attorney working on a fee basis would make more money if it took a long time to find a solution. True—it might be a better solution, but the improvement may not be worth as much as the cost of the extra fees, so that you have to balance your solutional drive with the attorney's personal drive. When you run into this problem, see what you can do to satisfy the attorney's personal needs for more fees. It may be the promise of more business in the future if they can wrap it up quickly, or if the attorney is being difficult, you may have to revert to a competitive drive.

Another example of personal drive would be a union negotiator who wants to look good to his members. He may see it as in his best interests to make an outrageous initial demand. Then he can go back to his members and say, "I wasn't able to get you everything you wanted, but just listen to their opening negotiating position. I was able to get them all the way down from that for you." If he had taken a more modest opening negotiating position, it might have been difficult to sell it to his members, because they might not feel their union fought hard enough for them.

Another example of personal drive would be a young buyer who wants to look good to his company. He may have put a great deal of time and energy in his negotiation, so the last thing he wants to do is go back empty-handed, without a signed contract. If your own drive is competitive, your best strategy might be to establish that the buyer has a time deadline and stall negotiations until the last moment. You might be able to reach a terrific settlement in the limousine on the way to the airport if he'd rather agree to anything than go home empty-handed.

There is also the *organizational drive*. You may find yourself in a situation where the buyer seems to have a fine solutional drive. She really wants to find the best solution, but it has to be a solution that she can sell to her organization. Therefore her drive has to be organizational. Even if she found the perfect solution, could she sell it to her people?

This happens a great deal in Congress, where the congressperson is eager for a sensible compromise but would be ravaged by the voters in their district for making it; in close votes you'll see this all the time, in both houses. The politicians who have the support of their voters will commit quickly. Those who will be in trouble back home may want to support their party but are reluctant to toe the line. The party leadership counts noses to see how many votes are needed to win. Then they let their members who would be the most hurt by voting for the bill vote no. The ones who would be hurt least are led like lambs to slaughter and made to vote for the bill.

If you sell to the government, you run into the organizational drive all the time, because the buyer has to conform to the mechanics of the bidding process. He may much prefer your proposal but is obligated by the system to accept an inferior proposal from your competitor because they met the requirements of the bid and came in with a slightly lower price. The better you understand the buyer's system, how the bids are written, and how you can influence the writing of the bids, the more you'll be able to work with your buyer's organizational drive.

When you're negotiating with a buyer who must please their organization, they may be reluctant to lay out they problem for you, because it would seem too much like collusion. So you need to be thinking, who could be giving the buyer heartburn over this one?

Is it their stockholders, their legal department, or perhaps government regulations?

If you understand the buyer's problem, you may be able to make the solution more palatable to the organization. For example, you may take a more radical position with the other people at his company than you do at the negotiating table. In this way, your compromise has the appearance of making major concessions.

Once, a company hired me to help them when their assembly plant union went on strike. The union negotiators felt that the solution that they had negotiated was reasonable, but they couldn't sell it to their members, who were out for blood. We arranged for a local newspaper to interview the president of the company. During the interview, he expressed sincere regrets that he was caught between a rock and a hard place. The union couldn't sell the plan to its members, and the president couldn't sell anything better to his board of directors and stockholders. It appeared that the strike would soon force him to move production from that factory to their plant in Mexico.

The next day, the workers' spouses opened the newspaper to read headlines that said, "Plan to close; jobs going south." By that afternoon, the spouses had put enough pressure on the workers that they clamored to accept the deal that they had previously turned down.

If you are dealing with a buyer who has to sell the plan to their organization, you should always be looking for ways to make it easier for them to do that.

The *attitudinal drive* negotiator believes that if both sides like each other enough, they can resolve their differences. This kind of negotiator would never try to resolve a problem by telephone or through an intermediary. They always want to be face-to-face with the other person so that they can get a feel for who that person is, believing that if the two parties know each other well enough, they can find a solution.

Former president Jimmy Carter is very much an attitudinal negotiator. He initiated contact with the North Koreans when they were refusing to back down on their nuclear weapons program. In 1994, he met with Haitian general Raoul Cedras when the United States was right up to the brink of war with Haiti, and pleaded with President Clinton for just a few more minutes to reason with the general. When he finally reached a settlement, he invited that bloodthirsty dictator to come and teach a Sunday school class at his church in Plains, Georgia.

Quick Summary of Negotiating Drives

- The *competitive drive*: A "gladiatorial" approach, find out more knowledge and reveal less about themselves, distrusts anything a buyer might say, assumes there has to be a winner and a loser.

- The *solutional drive*: Believes both sides negotiate in good faith to find "win-win" solution, open to creative approaches without breaking their personal principles, everything is negotiable.

- The *personal drive*: Main drive is for personal profit or aggrandizement, makes outrageous initial demands, balance this drive initially with solutional drive and then revert to competitive drive as last resort.

- The *organizational drive*: A form of *solutional drive* that must be sold to one's organization, typical drive of government officials, must conform to mechanics of organization's bidding process, reluctant to lay out the problem, make it easier for a person with this drive to sell the plan to their organization.

- The *attitudinal drive*: Prefer face-to-face negotiations, believe they can find a solution if both sides like and trust one another, can lead to appeasement of buyer, make sure this approach is a two-way street and leads to a win-win solution.

The problem with this kind of negotiating is that it can easily lead to appeasement of the buyer. The attitudinal drive negotiator is so eager to find good in the buyer that he or she can readily be deceived. Certainly it helps that you and the buyer like each other, because it's hard to find a win-win solution otherwise. But this is a two-way street. While you are working to have the buyer like you, the buyer is working to have you like them. If you both like each other you are just as likely to make concession to them as they are to you.

Power negotiators know that something is far more important than having the buyer like you: you must create a solution that is in both sides' best interests. Then it's mutually beneficial for you both to support the buying arrangement and see that it flourishes.

In this chapter, I've taught you how the way Americans negotiate is very different from the way other nationalities negotiate. I've also taught you how to analyze the force that's driving the other side in a negotiation, because that is the key to win-win negotiation. In the next chapter, I'll teach you the characteristics of a power negotiator.

Chapter Eight

Characteristics of a Power Negotiator

You've probably heard the expression, "He's a born negotiator." I don't think that could be true, do you? Read the birth announcements in your local newspaper. You'll never read that a negotiator was born at St. Bartholomew's yesterday. It's a learned skill, just like everything else.

Personal Characteristics

Let's start with the personal characteristics of a power negotiator. To be a power negotiator, you need to have or develop these personal characteristics:

- The courage to probe for more information
- The patience to outlast the other negotiator
- The courage to ask for more than you expect to get
- The integrity to press for win-win solutions
- The willingness to be a good listener

Let's look at each of these.

COURAGE

First is the courage to probe for more information. Poor negotiators are always reluctant to question anything the other says, so they negotiate knowing only what the other side has chosen to tell them. Power negotiators are constantly challenging what they know about the other side and—what's more important—the assumptions that they have made. Based on that knowledge, you should adopt many of the approaches of investigative reporters. As you gather information, ask the tough questions—the ones that you feel sure they won't answer, even if they don't. You'll be learning by judging their reaction to being asked.

Ask the same question of several people to see if you get the same responses. Ask the same question several times during an extended negotiation to see if you get consistent answers. (In our next chapter, I'll talk about the importance of gathering information before and during the negotiation.)

PATIENCE

Second is the patience to outlast the other negotiator. For a good negotiator, patience is a virtue.

I remember going around the country on a press tour to promote my book on negotiating. A couple of times I showed up at television stations, and the interviewers said to me, "You don't look like a negotiator." I knew what they meant, and it didn't offend me. They thought I'd look tougher and meaner (perhaps from seeing movies about union negotiators).

Many people think of negotiators as tough, ruthless people who will pull any ruthless stunt to trick the other side into losing. Nothing could be further from the truth. Good negotiators are very patient people who won't let time pressure bully them into making a deal is not in everybody's best interest.

Remember, the Vietnam peace talks? Our negotiator, Averell Harriman, rented a suite at the Ritz Hotel in Paris on a week to week basis. The Vietnamese negotiator Le Duc Tho rented a villa in the countryside for two and a half years. With your government, your people and the world press breathing down your neck for results, it takes courage to show that much patience, but it's very effective.

. . . .

Good negotiators are very patient people who won't let time pressure bully them into making a deal is not in everybody's best interest.

. . . .

COURAGE

Third is the courage to ask for more than you expect to get. As I mentioned earlier, Henry Kissinger believes that effectiveness at the conference table depends on overstating one's demands. Apart from projecting the willingness to walk away if you can't get what you want, I don't think there is anything more important than understanding this principle and having the courage to apply it.

We lack courage because we fear ridicule. When I taught you about the bracketing gambit in chapter 1, I told you that your initial proposal to the buyer should be so high that it brackets your real objective. You should always advance your maximum plausible position. Sometimes that's hard to do. We often don't have the courage to make those way-out proposals because we're afraid the buyer will laugh at us. The fear of ridicule stops us from accomplishing many things. To be a power negotiator, you must get over that fear. You must be able to comfortably advance your maximum plausible position without apologizing for it.

INTEGRITY

Fourth is the integrity to press for a win-win solution. *Straight Up*, by James Ramsey Ullman, was an excellent biography of the mountain climber John Harlan, who died at thirty years of age trying to climb the Eiger, a mountain in the Alps, direttissima (straight up). In the preface, Ullman wrote, "Straight up is a way of serving a drink. It's also a way to climb a mountain and of living a life."

I believe that straight up is also the way to negotiate. Often you will be tempted by the opportunity to take quick advantage of a buyer who's in trouble. You'll be in a situation in which you know something that if the other person knew, they wouldn't be so eager to buy from you. Having the integrity to push for a win-win solution, even when you have the other side on the ropes, is a rare and precious commodity.

By this I don't mean making costly concessions to the other side because you're so charitable. I do mean looking for ways to make concessions to the other side that do not take away from your position.

BEING A GOOD LISTENER

Only a good listener can be a win-win negotiator. Only a good listener can detect the other side's real needs in a negotiation. Here are some tips for being a good listener when you are with a buyer.

Increase your concentration by thinking of listening as an interactive process. Lean forward. Tilt your head a little to show that you're paying attention. Ask questions; give feedback. Mirror what the buyer said. Avoid boredom by playing mind games.

Concentrate on what the buyer is saying, not on the style of delivery. Do this by picking the longest word in a sentence or rephrasing what they just said, because you can listen four times faster than the speaker can speak. You need to do something, or your mind will wander.

Increase your comprehension of what the buyer is saying by taking notes right from the start of the conversation. Take a large pad of paper with you. Head it up with the date and the topic, and start to keep brief notes of what's being said. Paper is cheaper than the time it takes to go back and get the details. This communicates to the buyer that you care about what they're saying. An additional bonus is that when buyers see that you're writing things down, they tend to be a lot more accurate in what they're telling you.

Next, defer making judgment of the other person until they're through. If you immediately analyze someone as phony, manipulative, or self-serving, you tend to shut them out and quit listening. So just hold off and wait until they're through before you evaluate.

Improve your ability to evaluate what's being said by asking the buyer to present their conclusions first. Then, if you don't agree with them completely, ask them to support their conclusions. Keep an open mind until they have. Be aware of your personal biases, and be conscious of how they're coloring your reactions. When you are aware that your prejudices are causing you to distrust the other party (perhaps you're a person who can't stand people trying to hype you) and automatically resist what they have to say, whether it's right or wrong, be aware of that: it improves your ability to evaluate what they're saying. Take notes with a divided notepad, one with a line down the middle. On the left, list the facts as they were presented. On the right, note the evaluation of what was said.

A Power Negotiator's Attitudes

Now let's talk about the attitudes of a power negotiator:

- The willingness to live with ambiguity
- Having a competitor's spirit
- Not having a strong need to be liked

LIVING WITH AMBIGUITY

Power negotiators relish the idea of going into a negotiation without knowing whether they'll come out as heroes or carrying their heads in their hands. This willingness to live with ambiguity requires a particular attitude.

People who like *people* are much more comfortable with ambiguity; people who prefer *things* have trouble with it. For this reason, engineers, accountants, and architects—members of professions that depend on accuracy—have a tough time with negotiating. They don't like the push and shove of it. They would rather have everything laid out in black-and-white.

Let me give you a little quiz to test your willingness to live with ambiguity.

1. If you're going to a party, do you first like to know who's going to be there?
2. If your spouse is taking you to have dinner with friends at a restaurant, do you like to know exactly which restaurant you're going to?
3. Do you like to plan out your vacations to the smallest detail?

If you said yes to all three of these questions, you have a major problem with ambiguity. To become a better negotiator, I suggest that you force yourself to tolerate situations in which you don't know exactly what the outcome will be.

A COMPETITIVE SPIRIT

Good negotiators have an intense desire to win when they're negotiating. Seeing negotiating as a game is a big part of what makes you good at it. It's fun to walk into the arena and pitch your skills against the skills of the other party.

It always amazes me that salespeople can be so competitive in sports and so fearful when handling buyers. Say you enjoy racquetball, so you set up an early morning game with a buyer. You'll do everything you can within the rules of the game to beat them. Then you shower off and go to the office to negotiate the sale, and the moment the buyer mentions price, you roll over and feel you're at their mercy.

The more you think of negotiating as a game, the more competitive you'll become. The more competitive you become, the more courageous you become, and the better you'll do.

NOT NEEDING TO BE LIKED

Psychologist Abraham Maslow is famous for his hierarchy of needs, which he ranks as (1) survival; (2) safety, the need for security; (3) love and belonging, the need to be liked by others; (4) esteem, the need to be respected by others; and (5) self-actualization, the need to feel fulfilled. Power negotiators are beyond stage three. Most of the time they have surpassed the need to be liked.

Negotiation is, almost by definition, the management of conflict, or at the very least of opposing viewpoints. If you have an exaggerated need to be liked, you won't be a good negotiator, because you fear conflict too much.

Does this mean that good negotiators are ruthless people who win because they don't care if the buyer loses? No, not at all. It does mean that the most important thing to them is to hammer away at the problem until a solution is found with which everybody can live.

Beliefs of a Power Negotiator

Now let's talk about the beliefs of a power negotiator. There are five things that top negotiators always believe:
- There is always pressure on the other side.
- Negotiating is played by a set of rules.
- The word *no* is only an opening negotiating position.
- Acting dumb is smart.
- Concentrate on the issues.

PRESSURE IS ON THE OTHER SIDE

The pressure is always on the other person to compromise in the negotiations just as much as it is on you. But it never appears to be that way. You always think you've got the weaker hand.

For example, when you're walking into a bank to apply for a business loan, you may be intimidated. You look at that big bank with its glamorous surroundings, and you start thinking, "Why on earth would a big bank like this want to lend money to little old me?"

You lose sight of the pressures on the bank. This bank spends millions of dollars a year in advertising to entice you to come in for a loan. There is tremendous pressure on the bank to get their deposits out in the form of loans. Many people at that bank have jobs that depend on their making loans.

A good negotiator learns to mentally compensate for the belief that he/she always has the weaker hand. In the negotiations, as she strides up to the loan officer's desk, she thinks, "I bet that loan officer just got a royal chewing out from his boss, who told him, 'If you can't find somebody to lend money to today, we don't even need you around here anymore.'"

Why do you always think you've got the weaker hand when you're selling? Because you know about the pressure that's on you, but you don't know about the pressure that's on the buyer. Remember that the buyer is suffering the same fate. He knows about the pressure that's on him, but he doesn't know about the pressure that's on you. He's not going tell you this, but he probably feels that you hold all the cards. Typically, each side thinks that it has the weaker hand. Don't buy into it.

When a buyer says to you, "I've got half a dozen other guys that will do it for less money and do it just as well," don't buy into it. The buyer has pressure on

> A good negotiator learns to mentally
> compensate for the belief that he/she
> always has the weaker hand.

him just as much as you have on you. The minute you believe that and learn to mentally compensate for it, you become a more powerful negotiator.

PLAYING BY THE RULES

The second belief that makes you a good negotiator is that negotiating is played by a set of rules, just like chess.

Perhaps when you read my thoughts about gambits in the first three chapters, you thought, "Roger, you've never met some of the buyers I have to deal with in my business. They make Attila the Hun look like Ann Landers. They're never going to fall for that kind of thing."

That's fair enough, but I want you to buy a little blue sky from me until you've had a chance to try my suggestions out. Time and again, students have told me, "I never thought that it would work, but it did. It's amazing." The first time you flinch, nibble, or use the vise on the other person and walk out of the negotiations with $1,000 in your pocket that you didn't expect to get, you'll be a believer too.

I always remember training the employees of a large savings and loan in Southern California. At a local hotel, they arranged an afternoon seminar, followed by a cocktail party and a dinner. During the cocktail party, I was standing talking to the president of the savings loan when the maître d' from the hotel came up with two bottles of wine in his arms. He asked the president if he would like wine served with the dinner. He told the president that the wine cost $22.50 per bottle. The president was about to say, "OK" when I said, "You'll have to do better than that."

The maître d' looked irritated, and the president looked shocked. The maître d' finally said, "I tell you what: if you'll serve it for everybody, I'll give it to you for $15 a bottle."

The president's face lit up, and he was about to give his OK when I said, "We were thinking more like $10 a bottle."

This caused the maître d' to say, "I'm not going to negotiate the price of wine with you: $13.50 is absolutely the best I can do."

The president had been in the seminar that afternoon and had heard me talking about the vise gambit, but until he saw it in action, I don't think he thought that it would work. So buy some blue sky from me until you get a chance to get out there and try these gambits.

As I said, you play power negotiating by a set of rules, just like chess. The big difference between negotiating in chess is that with negotiating, the other side doesn't have to know the rules. The other side will respond predictably to the moves that you make, not because of metaphysical magic, but from tens of thousands of responses over the years.

We know how the other side will react. Not every time, of course, but enough of the time to make negotiating more of a science than it is an art. Believe me when I tell you that negotiating is a game that is played by a set of rules. If you learn the rules well, you can play the game well.

NO IS SIMPLY A POSITION

To power negotiators, the word *no* is simply an opening negotiating position. It's never a refusal. Remember that the next time you take a proposal into a buyer, and he explodes with rage and says, "Not you again! How many times do I have to tell you that I'm happy with my present supplier? I'm not going to buy anything from you today, tomorrow, next week, or ever! Get out on my office and quit wasting my time."

When that happens, remember that a power negotiator doesn't take it as a refusal (although I know it's close). You should only take it as an opening negotiating position. Think to yourself, "Isn't that an interesting opening position? I wonder why he decided to start with that approach."

Take a lesson from your children. You can say to your child, "I am sick of hearing about this. Go to your room. I don't want to see you until morning, and if I ever hear about this again, you are grounded for a month." Does your child hear refusal? No. She thinks, "Isn't that an interesting opening position?"

ACTING DUMB IS SMART

When you are negotiating, you're better off acting as if you know less than everybody else, not more. The dumber you act, the better off you are (unless your apparent IQ sinks to the point where you lose all credibility). There's a good reason for this: with a few rare exceptions, human beings tend to help people that they see as less intelligent or informed rather than taking advantage of them. Of course, there are a few ruthless people out there who will try to take advantage of the weak, but most people want to compete with those they see as brighter and help those they see as less bright. So acting dumb defuses the competitive spirit of the other side. How can you fight with someone who's asking you to help them negotiate with you? How can you carry on any type of competitive matter with a person who says, "I don't know? What do you think?" When faced with this situation, most people feel sorry for the other person and go out of their way to help him or her.

Do you remember the TV show *Columbo*? Peter Falk played a detective who walked around in an old raincoat and a mental fog, chewing on an old cigar butt. He constantly wore an expression that suggested that he had just misplaced something and couldn't remember what it was, let alone where he left it. He succeeded by acting dumb. His demeanor was so disarming that the murderers came close to wanting him to solve his cases because he appeared to be so helpless.

I act dumb by asking for the definitions of words. If the other side says to me, "Roger, there are some ambiguities in this contract," I respond with, "Ambiguities, ambiguities. Hmm. You know, I've heard that word before, but I'm not quite sure what it means. Would you mind explaining it to me?" Or I might say, "Do you mind going over those figures one more time? I know that you've done it a couple of times already, but for some reason I'm not getting it. Do you mind?" This makes them think, "What a klutz I've got on my hands this time!" In this way, I lay to rest a competitive spirit that could have made a compromise very difficult to accomplish. Now the other side stops fighting me and starts trying to help me.

Be careful that you're not acting dumb in your area of expertise. If you sell computers, you're expected to know if they'll work or not. If you sell medical supplies, you're expected to know if your product will meet the buyer's requirements.

Win-win negotiating depends on the willingness of each side to be truly empathetic to the other side's position. That's not going to happen if both sides continue to compete. Power negotiators know that acting dumb defuses that competitive spirit and opens the door to win-win solutions.

CONCENTRATE ON THE ISSUES

Power negotiators know that they should always concentrate on the issues and not be distracted by the actions of the buyer.

Have you ever watched tennis on television? Good tennis players understand that only one thing affects the outcome of the game: the movement of the ball across the net. What the other player is doing doesn't affect the outcome. Tennis players learn to concentrate on the ball, not on the other person.

When you're negotiating, the ball is the movement of the goal: concessions across the negotiating table. It's the only thing that affects the outcome of the game, but it's easy to get thrown off by what the buyer does.

Once I wanted to buy a large real estate project in Signal Hill, California, that comprised eighteen four-unit buildings. I knew that I had to get the price down far below the $1.8 million that the sellers were asking for the property, which was owned free and clear by a large group of investors. A real estate agent had brought it to my attention, so I felt obligated to let him present the first offer, reserving the right to go back and negotiate directly with the sellers if he wasn't able to get my $1.2 million offer accepted.

The last thing in the world the agent wanted to do was present an offer at $1.2 million—$600,000 below the asking price—but I finally convinced him to give it a try. He went to present the offer. By doing that, he made a tactical error. He shouldn't have gone to them. He should have had them come to him. You always have more control when you're negotiating in your power base than if you go to their power base. He came back a few hours later, and I asked him, "How did it go?"

"It was awful. Just awful. I'm so embarrassed. I got into this large conference room, and all of the principals had come in for the reading of the offer. They brought with them their attorney, their CPA, and their broker. I was planning to do the silent close on them." (This is to read the offer and then be quiet. The next person who talks in the negotiations loses.) "The problem was, there wasn't any silence. I got down to the $1.2 million and they said, 'Wait a minute. You're coming in $600,000 low. We're insulted.' Then they all got up and stormed out of the room."

"Nothing else happened?"

"A couple of the principals stopped in the doorway on the way out, and they said, 'We're not going to come down to a penny less than $1.5 million.' It was just awful. Please don't ever ask me to present an offer that low again."

"Wait a minute," I said. "You mean to tell me that in five minutes, you got them to come down $300,000, and you feel bad about the way the negotiations went?"

See how easy it is to get thrown off by what the other people are doing rather than concentrating on the issue? It's inconceivable that an international negotiator would walk out of negotiations because he doesn't think the other people are fair. He may walk out, but it's not because he's upset; it's a specific negotiating tactic.

Can you imagine a top arms negotiator showing up in the White House and the president saying, "What are you doing here? I thought you were negotiating with the Russians."

"Well, yes, I was, Mr. President, but those guys are so unfair. You can't trust them, and they never keep their commitments. I just got so upset, I walked out of there."

Power negotiators don't do that. They concentrate on the issues, not on the personalities. You should always be thinking, "Where are we now compared to where we were an hour ago, or yesterday, or last week?"

Former secretary of state Warren Christopher said that it's OK to get upset when you're negotiating as long as you're in control and you're doing it as a specific negotiating tactic. It's when you're upset and out of control that you always lose.

That's why salespeople will have this happen to them: They lose an account. They take it into their sales manager and say, "We lost this one. Don't waste any time trying to save it. I did everything I could. If anybody could have saved it, I could have."

The sales manager says, "Well, just as a relations gesture, let me give the other side a call."

The sales manager can hold it together, not necessarily because she's any brighter or sharper than the salesperson, but because she hasn't become emotionally involved with the other side. Don't do that. Learn to concentrate on the issues.

In this chapter, we've talked about the personal characteristics, attitudes, and beliefs of power negotiators. Remember, there really is no such thing as a born negotiator. Power negotiating is a skill that you can master.

Summary of Characteristics of Power Negotiator

Personal Characteristics
- The courage to probe for more information
- The patience to outlast the other negotiator
- The courage to ask for more than you expect to get
- The integrity to press for win-win solutions
- The willingness to be a good listener

A Power Negotiator's Attitudes
- The willingness to live with ambiguity
- Having a competitor's spirit
- Not having a strong need to be liked

Beliefs of a Power Negotiator
- There is always pressure on the other side.
- Negotiating is played by a set of rules.
- The word *no* is only an opening negotiating position.
- Acting dumb is smart.
- Concentrate on the issues.

In the next chapter, we'll talk about some of the pressure points that always affect the outcome of the negotiation: time pressure, information power, and walkaway power.

Chapter Nine

Pressure Points

I n this chapter, we'll talk about three pressure points that always affect the outcome of the negotiation: time pressure, information power, and walkaway power.

Time Pressure

Under time pressure, people become more flexible making concessions that they wouldn't otherwise make. Your children know this, don't they? When does your child ask you for something? Just as you are rushing out of the house, right?

When my son, John, was younger, I would get him to drive me over to Los Angeles Airport, which is about an hour's drive from my home in La Habra Heights. We wouldn't talk about anything of consequence on the way, but when we were curbside, my luggage was on the cart, and I was about to race off to catch the plane, he would suddenly say, "Dad, I'm sorry. I forgot. I need $50 to fix the muffler on my car."

"John, don't do this to me," I would say. "I teach this stuff. How come this didn't come up before?"

"I'm sorry, Dad, but I have a fix-it ticket. I must get it fixed before you get back from your speaking tour. So please, can I have the money now? I'll tell you about it next weekend."

After years of dealing with adults, children have instinctively learned that under time pressure, people become more flexible.

The rule in negotiating is the Pareto principle: 80 percent of the concessions come down in the last 20 percent of the time available. If demands are presented early in the negotiation, neither side may be willing to make concessions, and the entire transaction might fall apart. If, on the other hand, additional demands or problem surface in the last 20 percent of the time available, both sides are more willing to make concessions.

Think of the last time you bought a piece of real estate. It probably took about ten weeks from the time you signed the initial contract to the time you became owner of the property. Now think of the concessions that each side made. Isn't it true that during the last two weeks, when things came out to be renegotiated, both sides became more flexible?

Some buyers are unethical enough to use this pressure point against you. They wait until the last minute to bring up elements of the negotiation that they could have brought up earlier and resolved simply. Then, when you're getting ready to finalize the arrangements, the buyer puts these problems on the table because he or she knows that you'll be more flexible under time pressure.

This teaches you that you should always tie up all the details up front. Don't leave anything to, "Oh well, we can work that out later," because a matter that appears to be of little importance up front can become a very big problem. Under time pressure, you may ask the buyer, "Will you need barcode packaging on these?"

The buyer dismisses the question with a wave of the hand, saying, "That's not a big problem; we can work that out later."

It may not be a big problem now, but it could become a big problem later, when you're under time pressure to get the order shipped.

Why expose yourself to that kind of problem? Tie up all the details up front. When the other side says to you, "We can work that out later. It's not going to be a big problem," bells should start to ring and lights should start to flash. Don't let the buyer do that to you.

When you're negotiating, never reveal that you have a deadline. Let's say, for example, that you sell institutional furniture and have flown to Dallas to close a sale with a hotel developer. You have a return flight at six o'clock. You're eager to catch that flight, but don't let the buyer know. If he does know you have a six o'clock flight, let him know that you also have a nine o'clock backup flight, or for that matter, that you can stay over for as long as it takes to work out a mutually satisfactory arrangement. If they know that you're under time pressure, they could delay the bulk of the negotiations until the last possible minute. Under that kind of pressure, there's a real danger that you'll give things away.

Here's another aspect of time pressure: the longer you can keep the other side involved in the negotiation, the more likely they are to move around to your point of view. The next time you're with a buyer and you're beginning to think that you'll never budge them, think of the tugboats in the Hudson River off Manhattan. A tiny tugboat can move a huge ocean liner around a little bit at a time. However, if the tugboat captain backed off, revved up its engines, and tried to force the ocean liner around, it wouldn't do any good.

Some people negotiate like that. They reach an impasse in the negotiations that frustrates them. Then they get impatient and try to force the other side to change their mind. Think of that tugboat instead: a little bit at a time can move the liner around. If you have enough patience, you can change anybody's mind a little bit at a time.

Unfortunately, this works both ways: the longer you spend in a negotiation, the more likely you are to make concessions. You may have flown to San Francisco to negotiate a large sale. At eight o'clock the next morning, you're in their office, feeling bright, fresh,

. . . .

The longer you can keep the other side involved
in the negotiation, the more likely they are
to move around to your point of view.

. . . .

and determined to hang in and accomplish all of your goals. Unfortunately, it doesn't go as well as you hoped. The morning drags on without any progress, so you break for lunch. The afternoon passes, and you've only reached agreement on a few minor points. You call the airline and reschedule for the midnight red-eye flight. You break for supper, come back determined to get something done.

Look out: unless you're very careful, by ten o'clock, you'll start making concessions that you never intended to make when you started that morning. Why does it work that way? Because your subconscious mind is now screaming at you: "You can't walk away from this empty-handed after all the time and effort you've spent on it. You have to be able to put something together."

Whenever you pass the point where you are prepared to walk away, you have set yourself up to lose in the negotiations. A power negotiator knows to disregard any time or money that he or she has invested in a project up to any given point. The time and money are gone, whether you strike a deal or not.

Always look at the terms of a negotiation as they exist at any point and think: "Disregarding all the time and money we've poured into this up to now, should we go ahead?" Never be reluctant to pull a plug if the deal doesn't make any sense anymore. It's much cheaper to write off your investment than it is to plow ahead with a deal that isn't right for you just because you have so much invested in it. Forget what you've already invested and examine it if it still looks good the way things stand now.

Key points about time pressure

- Under time pressure people become more flexible.
- Don't let the other side know that you have a deadline.
- Remember the Pareto principle: 80 percent of the concessions take place in the last 20 percent of the time.
- Tie up all the details up front. Don't leave anything to "We can work that out later."
- Avoid time pressure unless you have options. Options give you power, and unless you have the options, you should avoid time pressure.
- The longer the negotiation, the easier it is to get concessions.
- Be patient, but be careful that you're not making concessions because you've put time in on the negotiation. Don't throw good time and money after bad.

Information Pressure

The side that has the most information can often dominate the other side. Why do countries send spies into other countries? Why do professional football teams study the replays of their opponents' games? Because knowledge is power, and the more knowledge one side can accumulate about the other, the better chance there is for victory. If two salespeople are vying for an account, the one who knows more about the company and its people stands a better chance of making the sale.

Despite the obvious importance of information, few people spend much time analyzing the other side before starting a negotiation. Even people who wouldn't dream of skiing or scuba diving without taking lessons will jump into a negotiation that could cost them thousands of dollars without spending adequate time gathering the information they should have.

ADMIT THAT YOU DON'T KNOW

Rule one about gathering information is, *don't be afraid to admit that you don't know.* In my seminars, I have the students break up into teams of negotiators, with some assigned as buyers and the others as sellers. I give them enough information to complete a successful negotiation. In fact, I purposely give each side discoverable strengths and weaknesses. I tell each side that if they're asked a question to which they've been given an answer, they may not lie. If they only unearth half of these carefully planted tidbits of information about the other side, they would be in a powerful position to complete a successful negotiation.

Unfortunately, no matter how many times I drill the students on the importance of gathering information— even to the point of assigning ten minutes of the negotiation for that alone—they are still reluctant to do a thorough job. Why are people reluctant to gather information? Because to find things out, you must admit that you don't know, and most of us are extraordinarily reluctant to admit that we don't know.

Let me give you a quick exercise to prove this point. I'm going to ask you six questions, all of which you could answer with a number, but instead of having you try to guess the right number, I'll make it easier for you by asking you for a range. So if I asked you how many states there are, instead of saying 50, you'd say, "Between 49 and 51." If I asked you how many miles it is from Los Angeles to New York, you might be less sure, so you'd say, "Between 2,000 and 4,000." You could say from 1 to 1 million and be 100 percent sure, of course, but I want you to be 90 percent sure that the answer falls within the range you give.

Here are the questions. Remember to answer with a range.

1. How many counties are there in the United States?
2. How many wives did Mormon leader Brigham Young have?
3. How much did we pay Spain for Florida in 1819?
4. How many Perry Mason novels did Erle Stanley Gardner write?
5. How many head of cattle are there in the United States?
6. What is the length of Noah's ark in feet, according to Genesis?

Here are the answers.

1. There are 3,042 counties in the United States.
2. Brigham Young had twenty-seven wives.
3. We paid $5 million for Florida.
4. Erle Stanley Gardner wrote seventy-five Perry Mason novels.
5. There were just over 91.9 million head of cattle in the United States as of January 1, 2022.
6. Noah's ark was 450 feet long. According to Genesis 6:15, it was 300 cubits long, and a cubit equals 18 inches.

Note that all the questions were obscure. There was no reason in the world for you to know the answer to any of them. By rights, you should have heard the questions and thought, "This is ridiculous. I have no idea." However, you probably went ahead and answered them anyway, because we hate to admit that we don't know.

So how did you do? Did you get them all right? Probably not, but think how easy it would've been for you to get them all right. All you would have had to do is to admit that you didn't know and make the range of your answer huge. You probably didn't do that, because just like everyone else, you don't like to admit that you don't know.

The first rule for gathering information is, don't be overconfident. Admit that you don't know, and admit that anything you do know may be wrong.

DON'T BE AFRAID TO ASK

Rule two for gathering information is, *don't be afraid to ask the question*. I used to be afraid to ask questions for fear that it would upset the other person. I was one of those people who would say, "Would you mind if I asked you how much money you made last year, or would you be embarrassed to tell me?" I don't do that anymore; I ask them. If they don't want to tell you, they won't. However, even if they don't answer the question, you'll still be gathering information.

Just before General Norman Schwarzkopf sent our troops into Kuwait in the Gulf War, ABC reporter Sam Donaldson asked him, "General, when are you going to start the land war?" I hardly think that the general was going to say, "Sam, I kind of promised the president that I wouldn't tell any one of the 500 reporters that keep asking me that question, but since you asked, I'll tell you that we're going in at 2:00 a.m. on Tuesday."

Of course Schwarzkopf wasn't going to answer that question, but a good reporter asks the question anyway. It might put pressure on the other person or annoy them so that they blurt something out that they didn't intend to. Just judging the other person's reaction to the question might tell you a great deal.

As I travel around the country, I'm always looking for bargains in real estate. Years ago, I was in Tampa had noticed a for sale by owner classified advertisement that offered a waterfront home on an acre of land for $120,000. To someone who lives in Southern Califor-

....
**There's one simple way for salespeople
to get information from buyers: ASK!**
....

nia, as I do, it seemed like an incredible bargain. If you could find an acre of waterfront land there, it would sell for many millions.

I called up the owner to get more information. He described the property, and it sounded even better. Then I said, "How long have you owned it?" That's a normal question that very few people would have trouble asking. He told me that he'd owned it for three years.

Then I asked, "How much did you pay for it?" That's a question that many people would have trouble asking, because they think it might upset the other person.

There was a long pause on the other end of the line. Finally, he responded, "Well, all right, I'll tell you. I paid $85,000."

Immediately I knew that this wasn't the great deal that it appeared to be. There had been a very flat real estate market in Tampa, and he hadn't improved the property. I learned a great deal from asking that one question. But what if he had refused to answer the question? If he told me that what he paid for it wasn't any of my business, would I still have been gathering information? Of course I would. What if he'd lied to me? What if he'd said, "Let's see, what did I pay for it? Oh, yeah, we paid $200,000. We were really losing money." If he'd lied to me, I would still be gathering information.

So don't be afraid to ask the question. It may seem incredibly simplistic to tell you that one way to get information is to ask, but all too often salespeople don't ask because they're afraid to or because they think they know the answer already.

I once spoke at a banquet for a large packaging company and sat at dinner between a sales manager and the vice president of a food manufacturing company that was the packaging company's largest customer. I was curious to know how much of the food company's business went to this packaging company. I leaned over to the sales manager of the packaging company and asked, "How much of their business does this company give you?"

"We don't know. They would never reveal that, but we do know they like to spread their business around."

A little later, I leaned over to the vice president of the food company and asked, "How much of your packaging business do you give this company?"

He said, "27.8 percent."

Surprised that he had told me, I said, "I thought you liked to spread your business around."

"We used to feel that way, but now if we find a supplier that will get into bed with us, we'll give them all of our business."

Here was valuable information that the man on my left would have loved to know but had never asked, because he didn't think the man on my right would answer.

What does this tell you? Ask even if you don't think they'll answer, and even if you think you know the answer, ask.

WHERE DO YOU ASK?

Rule three tells you that *where you do the asking can make a big difference.* If you meet with the buyer at corporate headquarters, surrounded by trappings of power and authority, it's the least likely place for you to get information. People in their work environment are always surrounded by invisible chains of protocol, what they feel they should be talking about and what they feel they shouldn't. In that environment, people are cautious about sharing information; get them away from that environment, and information flows more freely. I'm sure you agree that if you could get the buyer out to dinner or playing golf, they'd tell you all kinds of things that they wouldn't tell you in his office.

Fortunately, it doesn't take that much. Sometimes all it takes is to get that buyer down the hall to their company lunchroom for a cup of coffee. Often that's all it takes to relax the tensions of the negotiation and get information flowing.

Apart from directly asking the buyer, how else can you gather information about the company?, you can ask people who have done business with them already. Even if you think of them as competition, I think you'll be amazed at how much they're willing to share with you. Find out whom else the buyer does business with, and call that salesperson.

Another great idea is to ask people further down the corporate ladder than the person you plan to deal with. Let's say that you're going to be negotiating with someone at the main office of a chain of computer warehouse stores. You might call up one of their branch offices and get an appointment to stop by and see the local manager. Do some preliminary negotiating with that person. Even though they can't negotiate the deal, they can tell you a lot about how the company decides. Why do they select one vendor over another? What specification factors do they consider? What profit margins do they expect? What is the way they normally pay?

In that kind of conversation, be sure that you're reading between the lines. Without knowing it, the negotiation may have already begun. For example, the branch manager may tell you they never work with less than 20 percent profit margins when that may not be the case at all. Moreover, never tell the branch manager anything you wouldn't want him to tell the people at his head office. Take the precaution of assuming anything you say will get back to them.

GO THROUGH PEER GROUPS

Rule four for gathering information is to *go through peer groups*, because people naturally tend to share information with their peers. At a cocktail party, you'll find attorneys talking about their cases to other attorneys when they wouldn't consider it ethical to share that information with anyone outside of their industry.

Doctors will talk about their patients to other doctors, but not outside their profession.

Power negotiators know how to use this phenomenon, because it applies to all occupations. Engineers, controllers, foremen, and truck drivers all have allegiances to their occupations as well as to their employers. Put them together with each other, and information will flow that you couldn't get in any other way. You can take an engineer from your company with you and let your engineer mix with their engineers. You'll find out that unlike top management—the level at which you may be negotiating—engineers will have a common bond that spreads throughout their profession rather than just a vertical loyalty to the company for which they currently work. So all kinds of information will pass between these two.

Naturally, you have to watch out that your person doesn't give away information that could be damaging to you. So be sure you pick the right person, caution them carefully on what you are willing to tell the other side and what you're not willing to tell and on both your open and your hidden agendas. Then let them go to it. Peer group information gathering is very effective.

Key points about gathering information

1. Don't be afraid to admit that you don't know.
2. Don't be afraid to ask tough questions.
3. Get the buyer away from their work environment, and information flows more freely.
4. Use their peer group to gather information.

Walkaway Power

The last of the three pressure points is the most powerful: it's projecting to the buyer that you will walk away from the negotiation if you can't get what you want. In fact, if there's one thing that I can press upon you that would make you a ten times better negotiator, it's this: *learn to develop walkaway power.*

The danger is that there's a mental point that you pass when you will no longer walk away. You reach a point in the negotiations when you start thinking, "I'm going to make this sale. I'm going to get the best price and the best terms I possibly can, but I have to nail this one down."

The minute you pass the point when you are willing to say, "I'm prepared to walk away from this," you lose in the negotiation. So be sure that you don't pass that point. There's no such thing as a sale that you have to make at any price, and the minute you pass the point when you think there is, you've lost.

At seminars, when a salesperson comes up to me and tells me they made a mistake in negotiations, this is always part of the problem: they passed the point where they were prepared to walk away. Somewhere down the line in relating the story, they'll say to me, "I made up my mind that I was going to get it," and I know that was the turning point in the negotiations. It was the point at which they lost.

Many years ago, my daughter bought her first car. She went down to the dealer and test-drove a fine used car. She fell in love with the car, and they knew it. Then she came back, and she wanted me to go back down with her to renegotiate a better price. Tough situation, right? On the way down there, I said, "Julia, are you prepared to come home tonight without the car?"

"No, I'm not. I want it."

"Julia, you might as well get your checkbook out and give them what they're asking, because you've already set yourself up to lose in the negotiations. We've got to be prepared to walk away."

We walked out of the showroom twice in the two hours that we spent negotiating and bought the car for $2,000 less than she would have paid for it. How much money was she making while she was negotiating? (Bear in mind that I waived my normal fee.) She was making $1,000 an hour. We'd all go to work for $1,000 an hour, wouldn't we? You can't make money faster than you can when you're negotiating.

You become a power negotiator when you learn to project to the other side that you will walk away from the job if you can't get what you want. Be sure that you've built up enough desire in the buyer before you threaten to walk away. Obviously, if they don't want your product or service yet and you threaten to walk away, you're going to find yourself standing on the sidewalk, saying, "What happened?"

You should consider selling as a four-step process:

1. Prospecting: Looking for people who want to do business with you.

2. Qualifying: Can they afford to do business with you?

3. Desire building: Making them want your product or service.

4. Closing: Getting the decision.

Walking away is a stage four gambit. You use it after you've built desire, and you're going for the decision. Please remember that the objective is not to walk away; the objective is to get what you want by threatening to walk away. Don't call me and say, "Roger, you'd be so proud of me. I just walked away from a million-dollar sale." As General Patton said to his troops, "Keep the objective clear. The objective is not for you to die for your country. It's for you to get the other side to die for their country."

In a heavy situation where there's a big sale at stake, don't threaten to walk away without the protection of good guy/bad guy (see the next chapter). Don't do it alone. You should have a good guy left behind. Then if you threaten to walk away, and they don't say, "Hey, wait a minute, where are you going? Come on back. We can still put this together," you still have a good guy left behind. He can say, "Look, he's just upset right now. I think we can still put this together if you can be a little bit more flexible in your pricing."

Power negotiators know that learning to subtly communicate to the other side that you are prepared to walk away is the most powerful pressure point of them all.

In this chapter, I've told you about three pressure points that always affect the outcome of any negotiation: (1) the person who is under the least time pressure will usually do best in the negotiation; (2) the person who has the most information will probably do best; and (3) the person who is prepared to walk away has the control.

Quick Review of the Three Pressure Points

1. The person who is under the least time pressure will usually do best in the negotiation.
2. The person who has the most information will probably do best.
3. The person who is prepared to walk away has the control.

In the next chapter, I'll teach you two powerful negotiating gambits that will give you a great deal of power over your buyers: higher authority and good guy/bad guy.

Chapter Ten

Higher Authority and Good Guy/Bad Guy

In this chapter, I'll teach you two powerful negotiating gambits that will give you a great deal of control over your buyers. They are *higher authority* and *good guy/bad guy*.

Higher Authority

You would think that if you are going out on a sales call, you'd be ahead to have the authority to make the decision in the negotiations. "I know what I'm doing," you tell your sales manager; "let me just negotiate the best deal that I can." But you put yourself in a weakened negotiating position. When you do that, you're better off not to have the authority. If you do have the authority, don't let the other side know about it.

Conversely, you probably get very frustrated by the buyer who claims that he or she doesn't have the authority to make a final decision. Unless you realize that this is simply a negotiating tactic, you feel that you'll never get to talk to the real decision maker.

When I was president of the real estate company in California, I used to have salespeople coming into me all the time to sell me things: advertising, photocopy machines, computer equipment, and so on. I would always negotiate the lowest price that I could by using all the gambits I've discussed. Then I would say to them, "This looks fine. I just have to run it by my board of directors, but I'll get back to you tomorrow with the final OK." The next day I would get back to them and say, "Wow, are they tough to deal with right now. I felt sure that I could sell it to them, but they just won't go along with it unless you can shave another couple of hundred dollars off the price." I would get what I asked for.

I really didn't need the board of directors to approve the purchase, but it never occurred to me that this deception was underhanded. I, like the buyers you deal with, see it as well within the rules of the game of negotiating. So when the buyer says to you that they must take it to the committee, that may not be true, but it's an effective negotiating tactic to use on you.

Let's first look at why you should use this gambit, and then I'll tell you how to handle it when the buyer uses it on you.

Power negotiators know that you put yourself in a weakened position when you let the other side know that you have the power of decision. You should always have to check with a higher authority before you can change your proposal or make a decision. Any negotiator who presents himself as a decision maker has put himself at a severe bargaining disadvantage. You have to put your ego on the back burner to do this, but you'll find it very effective.

The reason that this works so well is simple: When the buyers know that you have the final authority to make the deal, they know that they only must convince you. They don't have to work as hard to give you the benefits of their proposal, because once you've given your approval, they know they have consummated the deal.

Not so if you're telling them that you have to answer to higher authority. Whether you have to get approval from the regional head office, management partners, or board of directors, the buyer has to do more to convince you. They must make a proposal that you can take to your higher authority and get approved. They know that they must completely win you over so that you'll want to persuade your higher authority to agree to the proposal.

> When the buyers know that you have the final authority to make the deal, they know that they only must convince you.

Higher authority works much better for you when your authority is a vague entity, such as a committee or a board of directors. For example, have you ever actually met a loan committee at a bank? I never have. Bankers at my seminars have consistently told me that for loans of $500,000 or less, somebody at that bank can make a decision without having to go to a committee. However, the loan officer knows that if he or she said to you, "Your package is on the president's desk," you'd say, "Well, let's go talk to the president right now. Let's get it resolved." You can't do that with a vague entity.

If you use this gambit, be sure that your higher authority is a vague entity, such as a marketing committee or simply the people back at the head office. If you tell the buyer that your sales manager would have to approve it, the buyer's going to think, "If your sales manager is the only one who can make a decision, why am I wasting time talking to you? Get your sales manager down here."

A vague higher authority appears to be unapproachable. In all the years that I told salespeople that I had to run it by my board of directors, I only once had a salesperson say to me, "When does your board of directors meet? When can I make a presentation to them?"

At this point, you may be thinking, "Roger, I can't use this. I own a small company that manufactures patio furniture, and everybody knows I own it. They know that I don't have anybody above me with whom I must check."

Sure, you can use it. I own my own company too, but there are decisions that I won't make unless I've checked with the people to whom I've delegated that area of responsibility. If somebody asks me about doing a seminar for their company, I'll say, "Sounds good to me, but I have to check with my marketing people first." So if you own your own company, your higher authority becomes the people in your organization to whom you've delegated authority.

Buyers love to use the higher authority gambit on you, because it gives them power without confrontation. How can you get angry with the buyer when it's the committee that is so hard to deal with?

Counter-gambits to Higher Authority

Fortunately, power negotiators know how to handle this challenge smoothly and effectively. Let me give you the counter-gambits to higher authority. Your first approach should be to try to remove the buyer's resort to higher authority before the negotiations even start by getting them to admit that they could make a decision if the proposal is irresistible. The last thing you want is to take your proposal to the buyer and have them say to you, "Well, that's fine; thanks for bringing me the proposal. I'll talk to our committee or our attorney or the owners about it, and if your proposal interests us, we'll get back to you." Where do you go from there?

If you are smart enough to counter higher authority before you start, you can remove yourself from that dangerous situation. Before you present your proposal to the buyer, before you even get it out of your briefcase, you should casually say, "I don't mean to put any pressure on you." (This is called a *preparer*. You've just prepared them for pressure. You've given yourself permission to put pressure on them.) "I don't mean to put pressure on you, but if we're going to go ahead on this, we need to get it going right away. So let me ask you this. If this proposal meets all your needs, is there any reason why you wouldn't give me a decision today?"

It's a harmless thing for the other person to agree to, because they're thinking, "If it meets all my needs, no problem. There's loads of wiggle room there."

However, look at what you've accomplished if you can get them to respond this way. First, you've eliminated their right to tell you they want to think it over. If they say that, you say, "Let me go over it one more time. There must be something I didn't cover clearly enough, because you did indicate to me earlier that you were willing to make a decision."

Second, you've eliminated their right to refer to a higher authority. You've eliminated their right to say, "I want our specifications department or our purchasing committee to look at it."

What if you are not able to remove the buyer's resort to higher authority? In many situations, you'll say that to a buyer, and they'll reply, "I'm sorry, but on a purchase of this size, everything must get approved by the specifications committee. I'll have to refer it to them for a final decision."

Here are the three steps that power negotiators take when they're not able to remove the buyer's resort to higher authority.

1. **Appeal to their ego with a smile on your face**. You say, "But they always follow your recommendations, don't they?" That's such an appeal to their ego that the buyer will usually say, "I guess you're right. If I like it, then you can count on it." But often they'll say, "They normally follow my recommendations, but I can't give you a decision until I've taken it to the committee."

If you realize that you're dealing with an egotistical buyer, try preempting their resort to hire authority early in your presentation by saying, "Do you think that if you took this to your supervisor, he'd approve it?" Often, an ego-driven buyer will make the mistake of proudly telling you that they don't have to get anybody's approval.

2. **Get the buyer's commitment that they'll take it to the committee with a positive recommendation**. So you say, "But you will recommend it to them, won't you?" Hopefully they'll reply, "Well, yes, it looks like a good proposal to me. I'll go to bat for you with them."

Power negotiators get the buyer's commitment that they will go to the higher authority with a positive recommendation. There are only two things that can happen at this point. Either they'll say yes, they will recommend it to them, or they'll say, no, they won't. Either way, you've won. Their endorsement would be preferable, of course, but anytime you can draw out an objection, you should say hallelujah, because objections are buying signals. That buyer is not going to object to your price unless they're interested in buying from you. If they're not interested in buying from you, they don't care how much you're charging.

For a while, I dated a woman whose hobby was interior decorating. One day she excitedly dragged me down to the Orange County Design Center to show me a couch covered in kidskin. The leather was as soft and supple as anything I'd ever felt. As I sat there, she said, "Isn't that a wonderful couch?"

"No question about it," I said. "This is a wonderful couch."

"And it's only $12,000."

"Isn't that amazing? How can they do it for only $12,000?"

"You don't have a problem with the price?"

"I don't have a problem with the price at all."

Now why didn't I have a problem with the price? Because I had absolutely no intention of paying $12,000 for a couch; I don't care what they covered it with. But if buying the couch interested me, would I have a problem with the price? You'd better believe I'd have a problem with the price.

Objections are buying signals. In real estate, we knew if we were showing property and the people were oohing and aahing all over the place—if they loved everything about the property—they weren't going to buy. The serious buyers were the ones who were saying,

"The kitchen's not as big as we'd like; hate that wallpaper. We'd probably end up knocking out that wall." Those were the ones who would buy. Think about it. Have you ever in your life made a big sale in which the buyer loves your price up front?

Of course, not all serious buyers complain about the price.

Your biggest problem is not an objection; it's indifference. I would rather the buyer said to you, "I wouldn't buy widgets from your company if you were the last widget vendor in the world, because . . ." than have them say, "I've been using the same source on widgets for ten years, and he does fine. I don't want to take the time to talk about making a change."

Indifference is your problem, not objections. Here's a question: what's the opposite of love? If you said *hate*, think again: if they're throwing plates at you, you have something there to work with. Indifference that's the opposite of love—when they're saying to you, like Rhett Butler in *Gone with the Wind*, "Frankly, my dear, I don't give a damn." That's when you know the movie is over.

. . . .

For Power Negotiators, *indifference*
is your problem, not objections.

. . . .

3. **Now you can move to step three:** *qualified, subject to close.* The subject to close is the same one that your life insurance agent uses on you when she says, "Quite

frankly, I don't know if we can get this much insurance on someone of your age. It would be subject to your passing the physical anyway, so why don't we just write out the paperwork, subject to you passing the physical?"

The life insurance agent knows that if you can fog a mirror during that physical, he or she can find somebody somewhere who will underwrite the insurance, but it doesn't sound as though you're making as big a decision as you really are.

Here are some instances of the qualified subject to close: "Let's just write out the paperwork subject to the right of your specifications committee to reject the proposal within a twenty-four-hour period *for any specifications reason*," or "Let's just write up the paperwork subject to the right of your legal department to reject the proposal within a twenty-four-hour period *for any legal reason*."

Notice that you're not saying "subject to their acceptance": that's too broad. You're saying subject to their right *to decline the agreement for a specific reason.* If they're going to refer it to an attorney, it would be a legal reason. If they're going to refer it to their CPA, it would be a tax reason, and so on, but try to get it nailed down to a specific reason.

The three steps to take if you are not able to get the buyer to wave his or her resort to a higher authority are: (1) appeal to the buyer's ego; (2) get the buyer's commitment that they'll recommend it to the higher authority; and (3) the qualified, subject to close.

The Counter to the Counter-gambit

What's the counter to the counter-gambit? What if someone is trying to remove *your* resort to higher authority? If the buyer says to you, "You do have the authority to make a decision, don't you?" You should say in so many words, "It depends on what you're asking. There's a point at which I may have to go to my marketing committee."

Let's say that you're selling aluminum garden sheds to a chain of warehouse hardware centers, and they're asking you to participate in their holiday weekend mailer. Your sales manager has set aside $30,000 for this, but the buyer at the chain is asking you to commit $35,000. You should shake your head and say, "Wow! That's a lot more than I expected. I'd have to take that to the advertising committee. I'd feel comfortable giving you a go-ahead of $25,000, but anything above that, and I'd have to hold off until I could find out what the committee has to say without creating a confrontation." You've put the buyer in a position where they might prefer to go with the $25,000 rather than have the entire mailing on hold until you can get back to them.

Notice that you've also bracketed his proposal, as I taught you in chapter 1. Assume that you'll end up splitting the difference. Then you'll still be within budget.

One more thing about the higher authority gambit: what if somebody is trying to force you to a decision before you are ready to make it? Let's say that a buyer is pressuring you to commit to price and sums on a shipment, but wants a decision right now. He's saying, "Harry, I love you like a brother, but I'm running a business, not a religion. Give me what I need on this one right now, or I'll have to go with your competitor."

How do you handle it? It's very simple. You say, "Joe, I'm happy to give you a decision. In fact, I'll give you an answer right now if you want it, but I have to tell you, if you force me to a decision now, the answer has to be no. Tomorrow, after I've had a chance to talk to my people, the answer may be yes. So why don't you wait until tomorrow and see what happens—fair enough?"

Using and handling resorts to higher authority is very critical to you as a salesperson when you're power negotiating. Always maintain your own resort to higher authority. Always try to remove the buyer's resort to higher authority.

Good Guy/Bad Guy

Now let's talk about good guy/bad guy, which is one of the best-known negotiating gambits. I'm sure you've seen good guy/bad guy used in the old police movies. Officers bring a suspect into the police station for questioning, and the first detective to interrogate him is a rough, tough, mean-looking guy. He threatens the suspect with all kinds of things that they're going to do to him. Then he's mysteriously called away to take a phone call, and the second detective, who's brought

Key points to remember about higher authority

1. Don't let the buyer know that you have the authority to make a decision.

2. Your higher authority should be a vague entity, not an individual.

3. Even if you own your company, you can still use the resort to higher authority by referring down through your organization.

4. Leave your ego at home when you're negotiating. Don't let the buyer trick you into admitting that you have authority.

5. Attempt to get the buyer to admit that they could approve your proposal if it meets all of their needs. If that fails, go through the three counter-gambits: (a) appeal to their ego; (b) get their commitment that they'll recommend it to their higher authority; and (c) go to a qualified, subject to close.

6. If they're forcing you to decide before you're ready to do so, let them know that the answer will be no unless they give you time to check with your people.

in to look after the prisoner while the first one's away, is the warmest, nicest guy in the world. He sits down and make friends with prisoner. He gives him a cigarette and says, "Listen, kid, it's really not as bad as all that. I've kind of taken a liking into you, and I know the ropes around here. Why don't you let me see what I can do for you with them?" (It's a real temptation to think that the good guy's on your side when of course he really isn't.) Then the good guy would go ahead and close on what salespeople would recognize as a minor point close. He tells the prisoner, "All the detectives really need to know is, where did you buy the gun?" What they really want to know is, where did you hide the body? But starting out with a minor point like that and then moving up from there works very well, doesn't it?

The minor point close is the car salesperson who says to you, "If you did invest in in this car, would you get the blue or the gray? Would you want the vinyl upholstery or the leather?" Little decisions lead up to big decisions. It's the real estate person who says, "If you did invest in this home, how would you arrange the furniture in the living room?" Or, "Which of these bedrooms would be the nursery for your new baby?" Little decisions lead up to big decisions.

Buyers work good guy/bad guy on you much more than you might believe. Look out for it whenever you find yourself dealing with two people: chances are you'll see it being used on you in one form or another. For example, you may sell corporate health insurance plans for an HMO, and you've made an appointment to meet with the vice president of human resources at a company. When the secretary leads you in to meet with the vice president, you are surprised that the president of the company wants to sit in and listen. That's negotiating two on one, which is not good, but you go ahead, and everything seems to be going along fine, so you feel that you have a good chance of closing the sale, until the president suddenly gets irritated. Eventually he says to his vice president, "Look, I don't think these people are interested in making a serious proposal to us. I'm sorry, but I've got things to do," and then he storms out of the room. This really shakes you up if you're not used to negotiating.

Then the vice president says, "Wow! Sometimes he gets that way, but I really like the plan that you presented, and I think we can still work this out. If you could be a little bit more flexible on your price, I think we can still put it together. Tell you what. Why don't you let me see what I can do for you with him?"

If you don't realize what they're doing to you, you'll hear yourself saying something like, "What do you think the president would agree to?" Then it won't be long before you'll have the vice president negotiating for you, and she is not even on your side.

If you think I'm exaggerating on this one, consider this. Haven't you at one time or another said to a car salesperson, "What do you think you could get your sales manager to agree to?"—as if the salesperson is on your side, not on theirs? Haven't we all at one time been buying real estate and have found the property we want to buy? We say to the agent that has been helping us find the property, "What do you think the sellers would take?" Whom is your agent working for? Who's paying them? It's not you, is it? They're working for the seller, and yet they've effectively played good guy/bad guy with us. Look out for it, because you can run into it a lot.

Counter-gambits to Good Guy/Bad Guy

Power negotiators use several counter-gambits to good guy/bad guy.

1. **Simply identify the gambit**. Although there are many other ways to handle a problem, this one is so effective that it's probably the only one you need to know. Good guy/bad guy is so well known that it embarrasses people to be caught using it. When you notice the other side using it, you should smile and say, "Oh, come on. You aren't going to play good guy/bad guy with me, are you? Come on, sit down. Let's work this thing out." Usually their embarrassment will cause them to retreat from the position.

2. **You could respond by creating a bad guy of your own**. Tell them that you'd love to do what they want, but the people back at head office are obsessed with sticking to the program. You can always make a fictitious bad guy appear more unyielding than a bad guy who is present at the negotiation.

3. **You could go over their heads to the supervisor**. For example, if you're dealing with a buyer and head buyer in a distributorship, you might call the owner and say, "Your buyers were playing good guy/bad guy with me; you don't approve of that kind of thing, do you?" But be reluctant to go over the buyer's head, because it can cause bad feelings that may create some real problems for you.

4. **Sometimes just letting the bad guy talk resolves the problem, especially if he's being obnoxious**. Eventually his own people will get tired of hearing it and tell them knock it off.

5. **You can counter a good guy/bad guy by saying to the good guy, "Look, I understand what you two are doing to me. From now on, anything that he says, I'm going to attribute to you also."** Now you have two bad guys to deal with, so it defuses the gambit. Sometimes just identifying them both in your own mind as bad guys will handle the problem without requiring you to come out and accuse them.

6. **If the other side shows up with an attorney or comptroller who is clearly there to play bad guy, jump right in and force their role**. Say to them, "I'm sure you're here to play the bad guy, but let's not take that approach. I'm as eager to find a solution to this situation as you are, so why don't we all take a win-win approach? Fair enough?" This really takes the wind out of their sails.

This gambit is very effective even when everybody knows what's going on. It was how presidents Carter and Reagan got the hostages out of Iran in 1979–80. Carter had lost the election. He was eager to do something about the Iranian hostage situation before he left the White House and Reagan could take credit for their release, so he started playing good guy/bad guy with the ayatollah. Carter said, "If I were you, I'd settle this thing with me. Don't take a chance on this new team coming into office in January. My goodness, have you looked at these guys? The president's a former actor. The vice president is the former head of the CIA. The secretary of state is Alexander Haig. These guys are crazy. There's no telling what they might do."

Reagan, playing along with it, said, "Hey, if I were you, I'd settle it with Carter. He's a nice guy. You're definitely not going to like what I'll have to say about it when I get into the White House." Sure enough, we saw the hostages being released on the morning of Reagan's inauguration. Of course, the Iranians were aware of good guy/bad guy, but they didn't want to take a chance that Reagan would follow through with his threats. This demonstrates that these gambits work even when the other side knows what you're doing.

In fact, when you're power negotiating with someone who understands all of these gambits, it becomes more fun. It's like playing chess with a person of equal skill rather than someone whom you can easily outsmart.

In our next chapter, I'll teach you how to become an expert at resolving problems in a negotiation. What do you do when the negotiation's deadlocked, when you have the buyer close to giving you an order but they won't quite commit? How do you force them to decide?

Key points about good guy/bad guy

1. Buyers use good guy/bad guy on you much more than you might believe. Look out for it whenever you're negotiating with two or more people.

2. It's a very effective way of putting pressure on the other person without creating confrontation.

3. Counter it by identifying it. It's such a well-known tactic that when you catch the other party using it, they get embarrassed and back off.

Chapter Eleven

Resolving Obstacles

What do you do when the negotiation's deadlocked, when you have the buyer close to giving you an order, but they won't quite commit? How do you force them to decide?

If you are a big-ticket salesperson, you will frequently encounter impasses, stalemates, and deadlocks in your negotiations with buyers. Here's how I define the three terms: an *impasse* is when you disagree on a major issue, and it threatens the negotiations. A *stalemate* is when you and the buyer are still talking, but you seem unable to make any progress toward a solution. A *deadlock* is when the lack of progress has frustrated both sides so much that neither you nor the buyer sees any point in talking to each other anymore.

Impasses

It's easy for an inexperienced negotiated to confuse an impasse with the deadlock. Let me give you four examples:

1. **The purchasing agent at an automobile manufacturer in Detroit says you'll have to cut your price by 2 percent a year for the next five years, or they'll have to turn to another source**. You know that it's impossible to do that and still make a profit.

2. **The buyer says, "I'd love to do business with you, but you charge too much**. I have three other bids here that are way below what you're asking." Your company's firm policy is that they won't let you participate in bid shopping.

3. **A buyer is yelling at you, "I don't want to talk about it**. Take the shipment back and give us credit, or the next person you hear from will be my attorney."

4. **The president of a plumbing supply company pokes his cigar in your face and growls, "Let me tell you the facts of life, buddy boy**. Your competition will give me ninety days credit. If you won't do that, we don't have anything to talk about." You know that your company hasn't made an exception to their thirty days net rule in the decades they've been in business.

All of these may sound like deadlocks to the inexperienced negotiator, but to the power negotiator, they're only impasses.

There's a very easy gambit that you can use whenever you reach an impasse. It's called the *set-aside gambit*, and it involves getting the other side to set aside the impasse issue and discuss minor issues first. By building momentum as you resolve the minor issues, you find that the impasse issue is far more resolvable than it appeared to be at first.

Use the set-aside gambit when a buyer says to you, "We might be interested in talking to you, but we have to have a prototype from you by the first of the month for our annual sales meeting in New Orleans. If you can't move that quickly, let's not waste any time even talking about it."

Even if it's virtually impossible for you to move that quickly, you should still use the set-aside gambit: "I understand exactly how important that is to you, but let's just set that aside for a moment and talk about the other issues. Tell me about the specs on the job. Do you require us to use union labor? What kind of payment terms are we talking about?"

When you use the set-aside gambit, you resolve many of the little issues first in order to establish some momentum in the negotiation before leading up to the big issues.

As I'll teach you in the next chapter, don't narrow it down to just one issue, because with only one issue on the table, there has to be a winner and there has to be a loser. But by resolving the little issues first, you create momentum that will make the big issues much easier to resolve.

Inexperienced negotiators always seem to think that you need to resolve the big issues first: if we can't get together on the major things like price and terms, why waste time talking about the little issues?

Power negotiators understand that the other side will become much more flexible after you've reached agreement on the small issues.

Key points to remember about handling an impasse

1. Don't confuse an impasse with the deadlock. True deadlocks are very rare, so you've probably only reached an impasse.

2. Handle an impasse with the set-aside gambit: "Let's just set that aside for a moment and talk about some of the other issues, may we?"

3. Create momentum by resolving minor issues first, but don't narrow the negotiation down to only one issue. I'll teach you more about this in the next chapter, on win-win negotiating.

Stalemates

Somewhere between an impasse and a deadlock, you'll occasionally encounter a stalemate. That's when both sides are still talking, but you seem unable to make any progress toward a solution.

Being in a stalemate is similar to "being in irons," which is a sailing expression meaning that the boat has stalled with its head into the wind. When you tack (which means to turn the boat across the headwind), you must do it with a smooth, continuous motion, or the boat will get stuck with its bow into the wind. No sailboat will sail directly into the wind, only at an angle to the wind. (If you want to park a sailboat, you simply turn it into the wind, and it will stay there.) If you lose momentum as you tack, there's not enough crosswind to move the bow around. So if you go into irons, you must try different things to get the boat to move. You may be able to do it by waggling the tiller or the wheel, or you may have to reset the sails to change the dynamics and correct the problem.

Similarly, when negotiations stall, you must change the dynamics to reestablish momentum. Here are seven things that you can do other than lower your price:

1. **Change the venue by suggesting that you continue the discussion over lunch or dinner.**

2. **Ease the tension by talking about hobbies or a piece of gossip that's in the news, or by telling a funny story.**

3. **Explore the possibility of a change in finances, such as extended credit, a reduced deposit with the order, or restructured payments.** Any of these may be enough to change the dynamics and move you out of the stall. The other side may be reluctant to raise these issues for fear of appearing to be in poor financial condition.

4. **Discuss methods of sharing the risk with the other side.** Taking on a commitment that may turn sour might concern them. Try suggesting that

one year from now you'll take back any unused inventory and good condition for a 20 percent restocking fee. Perhaps a weasel clause in the contract, which applies if the market changes, will assuage their fears.

5. **Try changing the ambiance in the negotiating room**. If the negotiations have been in a low-key, cooperative drive, try moving into a competitive drive. If the negotiations have been in a competitive drive, try switching to more of a cooperative drive. Consider how you could switch the stalled negotiations from one to another.

6. **Suggest a change in specifications, packaging, or shipping methods to see if this shift will make the buyers think more positively.**

7. **It may be possible to get the other party to overlook any difference of opinion, provided you agree to a method of arbitrating any dispute should it become a problem in the future.**

If you're team negotiating, you have a couple more options. First, change the people in the negotiating team. A favorite expression that attorneys use is, "I have to be in court this afternoon, so my partner, Charlie, will be taking my place." The court may be a tennis court, but it's a tactful way of changing the team. Second, remove a member who may have irritated the other side. A sophisticated negotiator won't take offense at being asked to leave, because he or she may have paid a valuable role as a bad guy.

When a sailboat is in irons, the skipper may know exactly how to reset the sails, but sometimes he or she simply must try different things to see what works. If negotiation stalemates, you have to try different things to see what will regain momentum for you.

Again, be aware of the difference between an impasse, a stalemate, and a deadlock. In a stalemate, both sides are still motivated to find a solution, but neither can see a way to move forward. The response to a stalemate should be to change the dynamics of the negotiation by altering one of the elements.

Deadlocks

If things get any worse, you may reach a deadlock, which occurs when the lack of progress has frustrated both sides so much that neither you nor the buyer see any point in talking to each other anymore.

Deadlocks are rare in the sales profession, but if you do reach one, the only way to resolve it is to bring in a third party to act as a mediator or arbitrator.

There's a major difference between an arbitrator and a mediator: With the former, before the process starts, both sides will have agreed that they will abide by the arbitrator's decision. A mediator doesn't have that kind of power. A mediator is someone brought in to facilitate a solution. The simply act as a catalyst, using their skills to seek a solution that both sides will accept as reasonable.

Inexperienced negotiators are reluctant to bring in a mediator because they see inability to resolve a problem as a failure on their part: "I don't want to ask my sales manager for help, because he'll think of me as a poor negotiator."

Power negotiators know that there are many ways a third party can resolve a problem. Here are some of them:

1. **A mediator can go to both sides separately and suggest to each that they take a more reasonable position**. An arbitrator can even force this by telling both sides to bring in a final solution within twenty-four hours, telling them that he will pick the more reasonable of the two proposals. This forces each side to be more reasonable, because each fears that the other side will present a more attractive plan. It becomes in effect a closed-bid auction of ideas.

2. **A mediator listens better to each side**. Mediators have less at stake, so they're not filtering the information through a prejudice positions. They may well hear something to which an opponent would be deaf.

3. **Mediators can persuade better because both sides perceive them as having less to gain**. You lose much of your ability to persuade if the listener sees you as having something to gain. For example, a buyer will believe you much more readily if you tell him that you're not on commission—and only the most naive voter believes a politician during an election.

Power negotiators know that there are many
ways a third party can resolve a problem.

4. **When negotiating directly, you tend to assume that if the other side floats a trial balloon, then they would be willing to agree to what they're suggesting.** A mediator can go to each side and propose a solution without implying that the other side is willing to comply.

5. **An arbitrator can get both sides back to the negotiating table without having to promise concessions.**

Both arbitrator and mediators can only be effective if both sides see them as reasonably neutral. Sometimes you have to go to great lengths to ensure this perception. Each side may insist on a team of three arbitrators so that each side selects one, and those two have to agree on a third. To ensure that they adhere to the highest ethical standards, they might all be members of the American Arbitration Association. The association has strict rules for the way their members can arbitrate and still stay within the law.

As a salesperson, you won't be going to that much trouble. Chances are that you'll be using a mediator, not an arbitrator, and that your mediator will be your sales manager or someone else from your organization.

If you bring in your sales manager to resolve a dispute with a customer, what is the chance that your customer will perceive him or her as neutral? Somewhere between nil and zero. Consequently, your sales manager must create a feeling of neutrality in the buyer's mind. The way to do this is for the sales manager to make a small concession to the other side early in the mediation process. The sales manager comes in, and even if he's fully aware of the problem, says, "I haven't really had a chance to get into this yet. Why don't you both explain your position and let me see if I can come up with a solution that you can both live with?"

This terminology is important here. By asking both sides to explain their positions, the mediator is projecting that he comes to the process without prejudice. Also note that he's avoiding the use of *we*. Have him patiently heard both sides out, then turn to you, and say, for example, "Are we being fair pushing that? Perhaps you could give a little along the terms or some other detail? Could you live with sixty days?"

Don't feel that your sales manager is failing to support you. He's trying to position himself as neutral in the customer's eyes.

Whenever you reach a deadlock in the negotiations, bring in a third party who's perceived as reasonably neutral by the other parties. Don't assume that you must avoid impasses, stalemates, and deadlocks at all costs. An experienced negotiator can use them as tools to pressure the other side. Once your mindset is that a deadlock is unthinkable, it means that you're no longer prepared to walk away, and you have surrendered your most powerful pressure point: walkaway power.

Remember these key points about handling deadlocks:

1. **The only way to resolve a true deadlock is by bringing in a third party.**

2. **The third party can act as a mediator or an arbitrator.** Mediators can only facilitate a solution, but with an arbitrator, both sides agree up front that they will abide by the arbitrator's final decision.

3. **Don't see the need to bring in a third person as a failure on your part.** There are many reasons why they can reach a solution that the parties to the negotiation couldn't reach alone.

4. **The third party must be seen as neutral by both sides.**

5. **If the third party is not seen as neutral, they should position themselves as such by making a small concession to the other side early in the negotiation.**

6. **Keep an open mind about the possibility of a deadlock.** You can only develop your full power as a power negotiator if you're prepared to walk away. By refusing to consider a deadlock, you are giving away a valuable pressure point.

Using Concessions

Now I'm going to teach you how you can cause a negotiation to deadlock because of concessions. If you are involved in extended negotiations over price, be careful that you don't set up a pattern in the way that you make concessions.

Let's say that you sell equipment, and you've gone into the negotiation with a price of $15,000, but you would go as low as $14,000 to get the order. So you have a negotiating range of $1,000. The way in which you give away that $1,000 is very critical.

There are four errors that you should avoid when making concessions:

1. **Making concessions of equal size**. This means giving away your $1,000 negotiating range in four increments of $250. Imagine what the buyer's thinking if you do that. They don't know how far they can push you. All they know is every time they push, they get another $250. They're going to keep on pushing. In fact, it's a mistake to make any two concessions of equal size. If you were the buyer and the salesperson made a $250 concession and when pushed, made another $250 concession, wouldn't you bet money that the next concession will be $250 also?

2. **Making the final concession a big one**. That would be the case if you made a $600 concession followed by a $400 concession, then told the buyer, "That's absolutely our bottom line. I can't give you a penny more." The buyer is thinking that you made a $600 concession followed by a $400 concession, so they're sure they can get at least another $100 out of you. They say, "We're getting close. If you can come down another $100, we can talk."

You refuse, saying you can't even come down another $10, because you've given your bottom line already. By now, the buyer's really upset because they're thinking, "You just made a $400 concession, and now you won't give me another lousy $10. Why are you being so difficult?" Avoid making the last concession a big one, because it creates hostility.

3. **Giving it all away up front**. A variation is to give the entire $1,000 negotiating range away in one concession. When I set this up as a workshop at my seminars, it's amazing to me how many participants will turn to the person with whom they're to negotiate and say, "Well, I'll tell you what he told me." Such naivete is charming, I suppose, but it's a disastrous way to negotiate. I call it unilateral disarmament. I don't think that's very smart.

You are thinking, "How on earth would a buyer be able to get me to do a stupid thing like that?" It's easy. They call you up and say, "You're one of the three vendors that we are considering.

You are way high right now. But we thought that the fairest way to do this would be to ask all three of you for a last and final bid."

Unless you're a skilled negotiator, you'll panic and cut your price to the bone even though they haven't given you any assurance that there won't be another round of bidding later.

Another way that the buyer can get you to give away your entire negotiating range up front is with the "We don't like to negotiate" ploy, accompanied by a look of pained sincerity on their face. The buyer says, "Let me tell you about the way we do business here. Back in 1926, when we first started the company, our founder said, 'Let's treat our vendors well. Let's not negotiate prices with them. Have them quote their lowest price, and then tell them whether we'll accept it or not.' So that's the way we've always done it. Just give me your lowest price, and I'll give you a yes or a no, because we don't like to negotiate here."

The buyer is lying to you. In fact, they love to negotiate. That is negotiating: seeing if you can get the other side to make a huge concession to you before the negotiating even starts.

4. **Giving a small concession up front to test the waters.** We're all tempted to give a small concession first and see what happens. So initially you tell the buyer, "I might be able to squeeze another $100 off the price, but that's about our limit." If they reject that, you might think, "This isn't going to be as easy as I thought." So you offer another $200; that still doesn't get you the order. So in the next round, you give away another $300, and then you have $400 left in your negotiating range. So you give them the whole thing.

You see what you've done there. You started with a small concession and built up to a larger concession. You'll never reach agreement doing that, because every time the other party asks you for a concession, it just gets better and better for them.

All of these are wrong, because they create a pattern of expectations in the buyer's mind. The best way to make concessions is to offer a reasonable concession up front, which might just cinch the deal. In this case, maybe a $500 concession wouldn't be out of line: half of your negotiating range. Then be sure that if you have to make any future concessions, they're smaller and smaller. Your next concession might be $200, then $100, and then $50. By reducing the size of the concessions that you're making, you convince the buyer that they have pushed you about as far as you can be pushed.

If you want to test how effective this tactic can be, try it on your children. Wait until the next time they come to you for money for a school outing. They ask you for $100. You say, "No way. Do you realize when I was your age, my weekly allowance was 50 cents? I'll give you $50, and that's it."

"I can't do it on $50," your child protests in horror.

Now you have established a negotiating range. Your child is asking for $100, and you are offering $50. The negotiations progress at a frenzied pace, and you move up to $60, and then $65, and finally $67.50. By the time you've reached $67.50, you don't have to tell them that they're not going to do any better: you have subliminally communicated that message.

Power negotiators know how to do even better than that. They know how to take away a concession that they have already offered the buyer, and I'll tell you how to do that next.

Key points to remember about concession patterns

1. The way that you make concessions can create a pattern of expectations in the buyer's mind.
2. Don't make concessions of equal size, because the other party will keep on pushing.
3. Don't make your last concession a big one because it creates hostility.
4. Never concede your entire negotiating range just because the buyer calls for your last and final proposal or claims that he or she doesn't like to negotiate. Taper down the concessions to communicate that they're getting the best possible deal.

Positioning for Easy Acceptance

The gambit of *positioning for easy acceptance* is very important, particularly if you're dealing with a buyer who has studied negotiating. If they're proud of their ability to negotiate, you can get ridiculously close to agreement, and the entire negotiation will still fall apart on you. When it does, it's probably not the price or terms that cause the problem; it's the ego of the buyer as a negotiator. You may not realize that just before you showed up in his office, she said to the person in charge of purchasing, "You just watch me negotiate with this salesperson. I know what I'm doing. I'll get us a good price."

Now she's not doing as well as he hoped in the negotiation, and she's reluctant to agree to your proposal, because she doesn't want to feel that she's lost to you as a negotiator. That can happen even when the buyer knows that your proposal is fair and satisfies her needs in every way.

When this happens, you must find a way to make the buyer feel good about giving into you. You must position for easy acceptance. Power negotiators know that the best way to do this is to make a small concession just at the last moment.

The size of the concession can be ridiculously small and you can still make it work, because it's not the size of the concession that's critical; it's the timing. So you might say, "We can't budge another dime on the price, but I tell you what: if you'll go along with the price, I'll personally supervise the installation to be sure that it goes smoothly." Perhaps you were planning to do that anyway, but the point is that you've been courteous enough to position the buyer so that he can respond, "Well, all right, if you'll do that for me, we'll go along with the price." Then he doesn't feel that she lost to you in the negotiation. She feels that she's traded off.

Positioning for easy acceptance is another reason why you should never go in with your best offer up front, because if you have offer at all of your concessions before you get to the end of the negotiation, you won't have anything left with which to position the buyer.

Here are some other small concessions that you can use to position:

1. A free training class on how to operate the equipment.

2. If you sell office equipment, offer to inventory their supplies and set them up on an automatic reordering system.

3. Hold this price for ninety days in case they want to duplicate this order for forty-five-day terms instead of thirty days.

4. Give three years for the price of two on an extended service warranty.

Remember, it's the timing of the concession that counts, not the size. It can be ridiculously small and still be effective. Using this, gambit power negotiators can make the buyer feel good about giving in.

Don't Gloat

Never gloat—never. When you get through negotiating, don't say to the buyer, "Harry, you know if you'd have hung in there a little bit longer, I was prepared to do this and this for you," because Harry's going to say unkind things about your mommy.

In the normal course of business, you'd never be foolish enough to gloat over the buyer for out-negotiating them. However, you can get into trouble with this one when you're negotiating with someone you know well. Perhaps you've been playing golf with this buyer for years. Now you're negotiating something. You both know you're negotiating, and you're having fun playing the game. Finally, he says to you, "All right, we're all agreed on this, and I'm not going to back out, but just for my own satisfaction, what was your real bottom line?" Of course you're tempted to brag a little, but don't do it. He will remember that for the next twenty years.

When you're through negotiating, always congratulate the buyer. However poorly you think the buyer may have done, congratulate them; say, "Wow, did you do a fantastic job negotiating with me! I realized that I didn't get as good a deal as I could have done, but frankly it was worth it, because I learned so much about negotiating. You were brilliant."

You want the other person to feel that they've won in the negotiations. Have you ever watched attorneys down at the courthouse? They'll cut each other to ribbons inside the courtroom. Outside, you'll see the district attorney go up to the defense attorney and say, "Wow, were you brilliant in there! You really were. True, your guy got thirty years, but I don't think anyone could have done a better job than you did." The district attorney understands that he'll be in another courtroom one day with that same defense attorney, and he doesn't want the attorney feeling that this is a personal contest. Gloating over a victory will just make the attorney more determined than ever to win the rematch.

Similarly, you'll be dealing with that buyer again. You don't want them remembering that they lost to you. It would only make them more determined to get the better of you in a rematch.

In this chapter, we've talked about what to do when you have problems negotiating with the buyer. You now know how to handle an impasse by using the set-aside technique. You know how to get stalled negotiations going again by changing the dynamics, and you know how to use a mediator if you reach a deadlock. I've taught you how to force a decision by tapering down your concessions and how to position for easy acceptance with a small concession.

Review of the Types of Negotiation Obstacles

1. An *impasse* is when you disagree on a major issue, and it threatens the negotiations.
2. A *stalemate* is when you and the buyer are still talking, but you seem unable to make any progress toward a solution.
3. A *deadlock* is when the lack of progress has frustrated both sides so much that neither you nor the buyer sees any point in talking to each other anymore.

In our next and last chapter, I'll teach you how terrorist negotiators use three stages to resolve hostage taking situations and how to structure win-win negotiations.

Chapter Twelve

The Win-Win Solution

In this chapter, I'll teach you how terrorist negotiators resolve hostage taking situations. You'll be able to use the same techniques to handle an angry buyer. Then I'll teach you how to structure a negotiation so that both sides feel that they've won.

Hostages and Angry Buyers

Let's talk about how to handle the angry buyer. Let's assume that something has gone wrong. The shipment was delayed. You accidentally overcharged them. They feel you lied to them. In any event, you have a furious customer on your hands. If you'll learn to go through the three stages that I'm going to teach you now, you'll find that frustration over this kind of problem is a thing of the past, and you'll be able to smoothly resolve the situation.

Several years ago, the mayors of the 442 cities in California asked me to teach them how to handle hostage negotiations. "Let's suppose," I said to them, "that you are the mayor of a small California city, and you've been called into a terrorist situation downtown. There's a gunman holding a gun on a hostage in one of your buildings. Your police chief is a little to the right of Genghis Khan, so he's in favor of blowing the whole place apart and killing everybody inside. Somebody hands you a bullhorn and says, 'OK, negotiate our way out of this one.'" (One of the mayors called out, "Wait a minute! I only got elected by forty-seven votes!")

Of course, it's unlikely that you as a salesperson will ever be in that kind of situation, but if you can learn to handle a hostage situation, you'll be able to smoothly handle an angry buyer.

ESTABLISH CRITERIA

The first stage is to *establish criteria*. Find out exactly what the other side wants to do, even when you are sure that you won't like what you're about to hear. Find out exactly what they want, even if you cannot or will not make any concession to them at all. Get them to establish their criteria in the terrorist situation. They might want five minutes on a local radio station. It might be a $100,000, or the release of some prisoners somewhere,

> Find out exactly what the other side wants
> to do, even when you are sure that you
> won't like what you're about to hear.

or it might be something that you are happy to give them.

When O. J. Simpson was fleeing police, he surrendered in return for a glass of orange juice and the chance to use the bathroom. In the 1993 siege in Waco, Texas, David Koresh wanted them to broadcast a tape that he had recorded. (I would have handled that differently. Instead of letting him give me the tape, I would have said, "David, we will do better than that. You come on down to the radio station and we'll let you go on live.")

A nationwide real estate franchise company hired me to teach power negotiating. At their annual meeting in the morning, they had an award ceremony for the top producers. As they finished handing out all these trophies and broke for lunch, I saw one of the branch managers come storming up to the front of the room. He grabbed hold of the vice president of the company and yelled, "You did it to me again! One of my top salespeople didn't get the trophy. How am I supposed to keep them motivated if you don't give them recognition?"

He must have caught the vice president at a bad moment, because he responded, "You know why he didn't get his trophy? Because you didn't turn your sales report in on time."

"Yes, I did."

"No, you didn't. You've been with us for five years now, and you've never turned a sales report in on time yet," and the fight was on.

The people who had lined up to talk with the vice president started drifting away in embarrassment, and I started to time this thing to see how long it would take the vice president to find out exactly what the branch manager wanted him to do.

Twenty-three minutes went by. By then, they were in a screaming match. The branch manager was saying, "I'm going to leave the franchise. I'm going to pull all my salespeople out. We are leaving."

"If that's all the loyalty we've got from you, we're probably better off without you!"

Here we have a major escalation of the problem, when all that it would really have taken was for the vice president to stay calm and say to the branch manager, "Wow! I'm sorry he didn't get his trophy. What exactly would you like me to do?"

The branch manager would have responded, "Give him some recognition during the lunch break or this afternoon, would you?" Then the vice president could have replied, "If I do that for you, what will you do for me? Can I get your assurance that your sales reports will be on time in future, so this could never happen again?" (That's the trade-off gambit that I've already taught you.) It all would have been over.

But we see that kind of escalation all the time, don't we? You walk into your office, and two employees are arguing about something over at the water cooler. They look upset, so you go over to see if you can help. When you find out what they're arguing about, you can't believe what a petty matter it is. One of them borrowed the other one's stapler and didn't return it, and the whole thing blew up out of proportion. Or in our personal lives with our spouses and children, something is said, the wrong response is made, and soon the whole thing has flared up, although we never meant for it to get that bad. We just don't know how to pull back from the positions that we've taken.

So that's always the first stage in any negotiation: we ask them exactly what they want us to do. Sometimes it's not as bad as we fear. At one point, a Lufthansa airplane was hijacked out of Frankfurt, Germany. The passengers thought they were going to get off in Cairo three hours later. Instead, they were hijacked, flown all over Europe, and then to New York and back. Finally, they were released. At that point, one of them spotted a Lufthansa official and went roaring up to him, furious. He had missed all of his business appointments in Cairo and had been terrorized for three days by what he saw as Lufthansa's lack of security. Imagine what must have been going on in this official's mind in terms of what it would take to calm this man down. Fortunately, he knew the rule: find out what they want first.

Do you know what the passenger wanted? Frequent-flyer mileage. That's all he wanted to resolve the problem. So sometimes it's not as bad as you fear, but even if it is, you're better off to get the other side committed to a position.

EXCHANGE INFORMATION

Stage two is to *exchange information*. Having established criteria, so that each side understands exactly what the other side is initially willing to do, we can go to stage two, which is to find out everything you can about the situation. This is one of the most critical parts of any power negotiation: to probe for more information. As I've already emphasized, information is one of the most critical pressure points. Here we see that it's the second stage of every negotiation. Find out all you possibly can. At this stage, don't jump to conclusions. Ask for information. In the case of the terrorist situation, we want to know if this person is a member of an organized group. Have they ever followed through on this threat before? What religion are they? Is there someone from the clergy we can call in? Where is their family? Who can we bring in to help us with the situation? We get all the information we possibly can.

Whenever you hear about a hostage negotiation where everything went wrong and people got killed, examine the news reports, and see if this wasn't the problem: the negotiators weren't able or simply didn't have the patience to find out more about the situation.

One day a man was walking down Rodeo Drive in Beverly Hills with a gun in his pocket. The man walked into Van Cleef & Arpels, the jewelry store, and pulled the gun out of his pocket. The guard on the front door locked the door of the store with all of them inside. Now here's a multiple-choice question for you: was that (a) dumb, (b) stupid, (c) idiotic, or (d) all of the above? I understand that they now have a sign on their lunch-room wall that says, "First you leave the store, then you lock the gunman in."

The Beverly Hills police, which trains by watching Eddie Murphy movies, called out every SWAT team in Southern California. Soon they had a gunman on the rooftop of every building and had this two-block shopping street completely barricaded off for three whole days. The merchants were going out of their minds. They were losing millions. They were passing the hat trying to raise bail for this man. On the third day, they finally had him in custody, but until they did, they didn't know his name. They hadn't gone through the information gathering stage.

REACH FOR COMPROMISE

So first you establish criteria, and then, in stage two, you exchange information. Only when you've completed these two stages do you go to stage three: *reaching for compromise* (which is what most people think of as negotiating). Start looking for things that the other party might see as of value and that you are willing to concede because they're not necessarily of value to you, and vice versa.

Follow these three stages of negotiation, and you'll see how formerly big, traumatic problems become easy to handle. Practice in little areas too. For example, before my son got his own car, he used to come to me and say, "Dad, can I borrow the car?"

I might immediately jump to the defensive without going through the stages. I'd say, "No, son, I don't want you borrowing the car tonight. We can't have you borrowing the car every night. You've got homework to do."

If I had gone through the three stages, I would have established criteria: (1) Find out where he's going with the car, and when he will be coming back. (2) Get all the information possible. Whom is he going to be with? If he's going to a movie, what movie is he going to see? (3) Reach for compromise that's acceptable to both of us, such as, "If you do your homework first, I'll let you go." Or possibly, "Tomorrow night, I'll take you to a movie."

Before I understood the importance of the three stages, I would jump to a conclusion, a big argument would start, and then I would find out that his mother had asked him to go down to the drugstore to pick up a prescription for her. Our relationship would have been weakened.

The next time you have an angry person on your hands, go through these three stages, and you'll be amazed at how things will drop into place for you.

Win-Win Negotiating

Finally, let's talk more about win-win negotiating. Instead of trying to dominate the buyer and trick them

The Three Stages of Handling a Hostage Situation (or an Angry Buyer)

1. Stage One is to *establish criteria*. Find out exactly what the other side wants to do, even when you are sure that you won't like what you're about to hear.
2. Stage Two is to *exchange information*. Find out everything you can about the situation.
3. Stage Three is *reaching for compromise*. Start looking for things that the other party might see as of value and that you are willing to concede because they're not necessarily of value to you, and vice versa.

into doing things they wouldn't normally do, I believe that you should work out your problems with the buyer and develop a solution in which both of you can win.

Now your reaction may be, "Roger, you obviously don't know much about the kind of selling that I do. I live in a dog-eat-dog world. My buyers don't take any prisoners. There's no such thing as win-win in my industry. When I'm selling, I'm obviously trying to get the highest price I possibly can, and the buyer is obviously trying to get the lowest possible price. How on earth can we both win in the negotiation?"

Let's start out with the most important issue: what do we mean when we say *win-win*? Does it really mean that both sides win; or does it mean that both sides lose equally? What if each side thinks they won, and the other side lost? Would that be win-win?

Before you dismiss that possibility, think about it more. Say you leave with a big order, thinking, "I won.

I would have dropped the price more if the buyer had been a better negotiator." However, the buyer is thinking that they won: they would have paid more if you had been a better negotiator. So both of you think that you won and the other person lost. Is that win-win?

Yes, I believe it is, as long as it's a permanent feeling. And, as long as neither of you wakes up tomorrow morning thinking, "Son of a gun! Now I know what he did to me. Wait until I see him again."

That's why I stress doing the things that service the perception that the other side has won, such as, don't jump at the first offer. Ask for more than you expect to get. Flinch at the other side's proposals. Avoid confrontation. Play reluctant buyer or reluctant seller. Use the vise gambit: "You'll have to do better than that." Use higher authority and good guy/bad guy gambits to make them think you are on their side. Never offer to split the difference. Always ask for a trade-off, and never make a concession without a reciprocal concession.

Here are some other fundamental rules to observe:

1. DON'T NARROW THE NEGOTIATION DOWN TO JUST ONE ISSUE.

If, for example, you resolve all the other issues and the only thing left to negotiate is price, somebody has to win and somebody has to lose. As long as you keep more than one issue on the table, you can always work trade-offs so that the buyer doesn't mind conceding on price, because you're able to offer something in return.

Sometimes buyers try to treat your product as a commodity by saying, "We buy this stuff by the ton as long as it meets specs; we don't mind who made it or where it comes from." They're trying to treat this as a one-issue negotiation to persuade you that the only way you can make a meaningful concession is to lower your price. When that's the case, you should do everything possible to put other issues, such as delivery turns, packaging, and guarantees, on the table so that you can use these items for trade-offs and get away from the perception that this is a one-issue negotiation.

At a seminar once, a commercial real estate salesperson came up to me who was excited because he'd almost completed negotiating a contract for a large commercial building. "We've been working on it for over a year," he told me, "and we've almost got it resolved. In fact, we've resolved everything except price, and we're only $72,000 apart."

I flinched, because I knew that now, because he'd narrowed it down to one issue, then there had to be a winner and there had to be a loser. However close they may be, they were heading for trouble.

In a one-issue negotiation, you should add other elements so that you can trade them off later and appear to be making concessions.

In August 1985, FBI agents arrested Gennadi Zakharov, a physicist who was a member of the Soviet delegation to the United Nations. The FBI had caught him red-handed as he paid cash for classified documents on a New York City subway platform. A week later, the KGB arrested Nicholas Daniloff, a Moscow correspondent for *U.S. News and World Report*. Nine months earlier, they had set Daniloff up by having a KGB agent dressed as a priest ask him to deliver a letter to the U.S. embassy. Now the Soviets were demanding the release of Zakharov in exchange for the release of newly arrested Daniloff, whom they had branded as a spy. Outraged by the blatancy of their move, President Reagan refused, and the incident began to threaten the upcoming arms control summit. Everybody knew that the fate of Zakharov and Daniloff was insignificant compared to the potential for world peace at the summit. But by now both sides had dug into their positions and were blind to their mutual interests. It was a one-issue negotiation: would we trade Zakharov for Daniloff or wouldn't we?

President Reagan was adamant that he wouldn't be a patsy for the KGB. To the rescue came Armand Hammer, the chair of Occidental Petroleum, who had been doing business in Russia since the revolution. He knew that the way to break the deadlock was to introduce another issue into the negotiations so that the Russians could offer a more palatable trade-off. He suggested to the Russians that they also agree to release dissident Yuri Orlov, and his wife, Irina Valitov. This broke the deadlock: Reagan, who had dug into his position of not trading a Russian spy for an American journalist, could find the new trade acceptable because it didn't violate his previously stated position.

So if you find yourself deadlocked with a one-issue negotiation, you should try adding other issues into the mix. Fortunately, there are usually many more elements than just the one major issue that are important in the negotiations. The art of win-win negotiating is to piece together those elements; it's like putting together a jigsaw puzzle so that both people can win.

So rule one is, *don't narrow the negotiation down to just one issue.* While we may resolve impasses by finding a common ground on smaller issues to keep the negotiation moving, as I taught you in the previous chapter, you should never narrow it down to one issue.

2. UNDERSTAND THAT PEOPLE ARE NOT OUT FOR THE SAME THING.

We all have an overriding tendency to assume that other people want what we want, that what's important to us will be important to them. But that's not true.

The biggest trap into which salespeople fall is assuming that price is the dominant issue in the negotiation. Obviously there are many other elements other than price that are important to the buyer. You must convince the buyer of the quality of your product or service. They need to know that you'll deliver on time. They want to know that you will give adequate management supervision to their account. How flexible are you on payment terms? Does your company have the financial strength to be a partner of theirs? Do you have the support of a well-trained and motivated workforce? These all come into play, along with half a dozen other factors.

When you have satisfied the buyer that you can meet all those requirements, then and only then does price become a deciding factor. So the second key to win-win negotiating is don't assume that the buyer wants what you want: if you do, you make the further assumption that anything you do in the negotiations to help them get what they want takes you further away from what you want. Win-win negotiating can only come when you understand that people don't want the same things in the negotiation.

Consequently, good power negotiating becomes not just a matter of getting what you want, but also being concerned about the other person getting what they want. One of the most powerful thoughts you can have when you're negotiating with a buyer is not, "What can I get from them?" but "What can I give them that won't take away from my position?" When you give people what they want in a negotiation, they'll give you what you want.

3. DON'T BE TOO GREEDY. DON'T TRY TO GET THE LAST DOLLAR OFF THE TABLE.

You may feel that you have triumphed, but does that help you if the other person feels that you vanquished them? That last dollar left on the table is a very expensive dollar to pick up.

A man who attended my seminar in Tucson told me that he was able to buy the company that he owned because the other potential buyer made that mistake. The other person had negotiated hard and pushed the seller to the brink of frustration. As a final nibble, the buyer said, "You are going to put new tires on that pickup truck before you transfer title, aren't you?" That was the straw that broke the proverbial camel's back. The owner reacted angrily, refused to sell his company to him, and instead sold it to the man in my seminar. Don't try to get it all, but leave something on the table so that the other person feels that she won.

4. PUT SOMETHING BACK ON THE TABLE WHEN THE NEGOTIATION IS OVER.

I don't mean telling them that you'll give them a discount over and above what you've negotiated. I mean, do something extra, over and above what you promised to do. Give them a little extra service. Care about them a little more than you have to. You'll find the little extra that they didn't have to negotiate for means more to them than everything for which they did have to negotiate.

Let me recap what I've taught you about win-win negotiating.

1. **Review chapter 6 again, on personality styles. Buyers have different personality styles, so they negotiate differently**. You must understand your personality style, and if it's different from the buyer's, you must adapt your style of negotiating to theirs.

2. **Different styles mean that in a negotiation, different buyers have different goals, relationships, styles, and faults, as well as different methods of getting what they want.**

3. **Winning is a perception**. By constantly serving the perception that the buyer is winning, you can convince them that they have won without having to make any concessions.

4. **Don't narrow the negotiation down to just one issue**.

5. **Don't assume that helping the buyer get what they want takes away from your position**. You are not out for the same thing. Poor negotiators try to force the buyer to get off the positions that they've taken. Power negotiators know that even when positions are 180 degrees apart, the interests of both sides can be neutral. So they work to get people off of their positions and concentrating on their interests.

6. **Don't be greedy**. Don't try to get the last dollar off the table.

7. **Put something back on the table**. Do more than the other party has bargained for.

If you do all of these things, your buyers will perceive you as a win-win negotiator.

Now you are ready to graduate as a power negotiator. The skills you've learned will give you the power to command any sales situation so that you can smoothly get the best deal for you and your company.

Far more importantly, these skills will give you the power to manage conflict in your life from now on. There should never be a time when you lose control of a situation because of anger or frustration. From now on, you will be in control of your life. You may let yourself get angry or upset, but only as a specific negotiating technique. You will never be out of control. Even when it's only a simple matter of getting your son to clean up his room or getting your daughter to go to bed on time, you will be in control.

From now on, you will understand that whenever you see conflict, it is because one or more of the participants does not understand power negotiating. Whether it's a husband or wife in an argument, a worker going on strike, a crime being committed, or an ugly international incident, power negotiators know that it has happened because the participants did not know how to get what they want without resorting to conflict. I look forward to the day when all conflicts are avoided because people know how to get what they want with good negotiating skills.

I invite you to share this vision with me by pledging now to remove conflict from your life and the lives of those around you. By always practicing good negotiating skills, the example that you set will help lead us into a bright new future, where violence, crime, and wars become a distant memory.

Now we've come to the end of this book. If you've been with me through all twelve chapters, you've just completed the most comprehensive program on sales negotiating available anywhere.

Congratulate yourself, because you have just graduated as a power negotiator. Good luck with all your negotiations!

....

"By always practicing good negotiating skills,
the example that you set will help lead us into a
bright new future, where violence, crime,
and wars become a distant memory."
—Roger Dawson

....